E N D

Read *Leadership Gravitas* like your life and leadership depend on it, because they do! Eric challenges us throughout the book to be daring enough to fight for a better version of ourselves. The principles and tools in this book are everything you need to develop your own Leadership Gravitas should you accept the challenge. I'm so glad I did!

KAREN BIEBUYCK
Founder and CEO of Strength Advisors
Gallup Certified Coach and Leadership Consultant

We've all been there before, fumbling around in the dark as we try to navigate the valleys of reality. At times, the journey feels so daunting, it seems the only sane option is to turn around and march back to a life that is comfortable, but stale. Our journey needs a guide, and not just any guide, but a guide that bears the fruit and scars from traveling the pathways we wrongly assume no one has tread before except ourselves. More than anything, we deeply desire to be empowered and equipped to live.

Without the compassion, investment and wisdom of Eric in my own life, a great deal of raw potential would be left unearthed in my being. If you're tired of hitting the proverbial brick wall, then the content in this read is your much needed wrecking ball.

LANDRY FIELDS
Assistant General Manager of the Atlanta Hawks and former NBA player

Once I started reading, I couldn't stop. This book is a reminder of not only who we are, but who we can be. As someone with a large team at work and at home, self-awareness and understanding of how to react and treat others is simply breautiful... yes, *breautiful*.

MITCHELL BAILEY
Creator/Co-founder Trust Me Vodka

A slam-dunk of an easy read and a provocative description of the complex world of coaching business leadership! Reading Eric Pfeiffer's book could be likened to going on a river rafting trip with him as a personal guide. His casual writing style easily carried me, his minimalistic diagrams concisely mapped out and reinforced crucial theory, and his personal life stories kept me actively engaged with the rigorous journey towards the acquisition of character or gravitas necessary for effective leadership. Bravo, Eric!

SHELLY ROYALTY
MDiv. PsyD

I have the great privilege of leading over 80 professional sales reps in the highly competitive world of medical device sales, specifically orthopedics. When the lockdowns began in April 2020, our salesforce were afforded time and opportunity to refine sales process and develop new skills. The top of the list was emotional intelligence, so we sought out Eric and MPWR to incorporate the EQ Matrix into our sales processes. The results were dramatic. We had almost zero attrition over the next year and our leadership gained a much better understanding of how to manage the critical challenges Eric describes as "pinballing." I highly recommend the book and more importantly, the author.

GRANT STONE
Vice President of Sales
MicroMed/Arthrex

If you know Eric, then you've experienced his empowering leadership. He lives out the concepts in this book with his family, friends and community. Anyone around him will be championed into their greatest potential. His vulnerable heart comes through in every page as he shares personal stories. This book addresses internal anxieties every leader experiences and helps you to embrace yourself as is. But he doesn't stop there; you will be taught how to identify and change restrictive thoughts and behavioral patterns that limit your influence.

Leadership Gravitas encourages you to look deep within as you discover the solutions to your challenges. In this book and in real life, Eric empowers people to feel known, understood and celebrated. He leads with playfulness, yet speaks piercing truth into the lives of those around him. This book is foundational for emerging leaders and for those who have been leading for decades.

MADI STONIER, LCSW
President of One Life Counseling

Leadership Gravitas... nothing can be more important for your personal development to make you the best leader you can be. Eric Pfeiffer nails it in this book with simple, concrete, yet profound ways to make a huge impact on how you function in your everyday life.

MATTHEW J. LOVINGIER
President
JMH Engineering and Construction

Eric's book provides quite a gift to leaders in bridging the gap from an academic discussion to every day practice. The EQ Matrix will be an invaluable tool to increase one's Leadership Gravitas if used diligently! This book is an important addition to Daniel Goleman's *Emotional Intelligence* book.

RICHARD MILLER
Ph.D., CEO-Retired

Leadership Gravitas provides a practical and engaging view of EQ. Eric is skilled with concepts, language and tools. In a subtle way, he offers a mirror so we can see ourselves and develop healthier leadership character, privately and in business. Then, he introduces the practical tool of the EQ Matrix so we can easily see what we are doing right in leadership and what adjustments will make life relationships richer.

Personally, some years back, with two 8ft x 4ft white boards, Eric walked my wife and me through a sober look at our life diagraming our activities including a start-up technology company, real estate, coaching couples, church leadership, volunteer boards, "special needs" and health challenges at home. The result of the tools he provided led us to change our life purpose statement and adjust relationships and priorities for a balanced life that both Bev and I enjoy significantly more.

Eric intelligently lays out the discovery process to being a more effective leader. He successfully brings a fresh and results-oriented approach to familiar and sometimes emotional topics. The insight and guidance offered in *Leadership Gravitas* provides a frame work for personal and business reflection that sets a trajectory towards healthy personal and business leadership growth. Keep reading, your future will be well rewarded.

Kai Ruud Adler
Entrepreneur, Speaker, Proctor Gallagher business/start-up consultant,
Marriage Coach - Married in Business, Non-profit advisor

Leadership Gravitas brings real world tools and personal insight into the emotional leadership EQ space. Eric mixes personal experience and leadership coaching together with a teaching mindset to provide a thought-provoking view of emotional leadership. As a reader and a student, you are challenged to use the tools provided to find your own Leadership Gravitas.

Erik Benjamson
Construction Executive

When I discovered I was passionate about leading others, I also discovered I didn't know how. I have become aware that it is my responsibility to lead myself well if I am going to lead others. The EQ Matrix tool rescues me from the pit of insecurity over and over, allowing me to develop a Leadership Gravitas that I can be proud of. It is one of my favorite tools I keep close. Thank you, Eric Pfeiffer, for making a significant impact on my calling by teaching me the EQ Matrix and more!

ROBERT RENTERIA

Founder and president of The Rockstar Platform

Refreshing and honest, *Leadership Gravitas* draws the reader into a journey of personal transformation. A key tenet woven into the book is that the development of Emotional Intelligence (EQ) provides the power to grow & improve leadership skills in both our professional and personal lives. This is brought to life through real world examples, stories, and testimonies and helps turn theory into practice. There are hidden gems throughout the book that capture the essence of EQ and offer guideposts for behavior. One of my favorites is, "You can only lead others to the degree that you lead yourself."

As a personal testimony, I have applied the key elements in this book and have been rewarded with greater confidence in my leadership skills and a feeling of empowerment to deliver work in new and exciting ways. This has helped build my relationship with leadership in the organization. I have been trusted to develop & launch a leader development program that was only a dream 18 months ago.

I can therefore highly recommend this book as a way to accelerate your learning on Emotional Intelligence and to inspire you to deliver your best work as a leader.

NICK HOPKINS

BSC(Hons), PhD, MBA

Senior Director, Executive Operations, Pharmaceutical Industry

ISBN: 978-1-7373414-0-6 (PB)
ISBN: 978-1-7373414-1-3 (eBook)

Printed in the United States of America

Published by Gravitas House

www.gravitashouse.com

Edited by Suzanne Lathrop and Tiffany Vakilian
Interior design and art by Olivier Darbonville
Cover design by Olivier Darbonville

LEADERSHIP GRAVITAS

12 Essential Skills to Expand Your Impact & Influence

ERIC PFEIFFER

ACKNOWLEDGMENTS

The endeavor of writing a book is too large for any single person to achieve alone. Everything I have poured out in this book is because of the many people who invested in, supported, challenged and believed in me over the many years. I cannot name them all, but you know who you are. THANK YOU a million times over for helping me become the person I am today!

A special thanks to those who partnered with me in the development, writing and execution of *Leadership Gravitas*. To name a few - Kandi Pfeiffer, Cody Miller, Jeff Waterman, Charity Pfeiffer, Alice Crider, Suzanne Lathrop, and everyone who was kind enough to give feedback along the way.

DEDICATION

———

This book is dedicated to my enduring wife, Kandi Pfeiffer. You believed in me when I have struggled to believe in myself. Your unwavering love, patience and timely "kicks in the pants" have urged me forward in my own journey of self-discovery. I owe much of my own leadership gravitas to your persevering partnership. Thank you, my love, for loving me so intensely and graciously. You are my rock! You make me better.

And to my two teenage children, Charity and Justus. No one has experienced more of the best and worst of my leadership journey. Your remarkable patience, forgiveness and encouragement has made being a father one of the great joys of my life. You are not only the fruit of my loins, you are also the fruit of my leadership. I couldn't be more proud of who you are. May my ceiling always be your floor.

CONTENTS

EMOTIONAL
INTELLIGENCE
AND PERSONAL
RESPONSIBILITY

AN INVITATION

We all want influence. And we should.

We want to be taken seriously—for our contributions to be seen as important. We all want our presence to matter, for others to respect us and value what we bring to any situation. We want our voice to carry weight. Whether in our home, in our friendships, on social media, or at work, we want influence. As we negotiate deals, lead a team, or engage in any conversation, we want influence.

Here's a truth no one ever told me. We all have influence, but it's not always valued. We all impact our environment, but not always in a way that is considered an asset. We can have influence by our passivity as much as our aggression. We can shape any situation with kindness as much as with anger and hostility. Whether in person, via text, email, or in a post, we affect the world around us every day. Think about it, you can post something today online that could significantly impact other people years from now. Wow!

The most important question is not whether we have influence, but whether others appreciate, value, and benefit from our influence.

A question I often ask myself is, "How are others experiencing my influence?" Even more importantly, I'll ask others, "How are you experiencing my influence?" It can be a very intimidating question because I know sometimes I'm going to hear things I don't want to hear.

But here's the thing, I've learned over the years that I'm not always the best judge of how others are experiencing me. I've been denied promotions, lost friendships, unintentionally offended others, injured my spouse and kids, led teams into disrepair, lost clients... All of this happened because I was unaware of how my influence was being experienced.

I spent years frustrated by failed opportunities and all because I had not yet learned the importance of developing my *leadership gravitas.*

My what?

Grav·i·tas (*grav-i-tahs*) is a noun that means seriousness or sobriety, as in conduct or speech.[1] Gravitas also denotes dignity, seriousness, or solemnity of manner.[2]

Gravitas was considered one of the most valued of the ancient Roman virtues. It described a person whose character and behavior carried weight, dignity, and importance. Anyone who

---

1 https://www.dictionary.com/browse/gravitas
2 Google Dictionary/Gravitas

was anyone back then wanted to be seen as someone who had gravitas. Because of their personal restraint, moral integrity and commitment to responsibility they were trusted by others. They were given leadership and were followed in times of crisis and turmoil.[3]

According to Sandra Zimmer, "Gravitas is a quality that a [person] exudes because she chooses to say and do only what is important. Others grant her respect and pay particular attention to what she says and does because she knows that she adds weight or value to any situation in which she speaks."[4]

I'm sure you've seen a movie with a character that carries gravitas. You might remember Gandolf from *Lord of the Rings* or Yoda from *Star Wars*. Sure, both characters have their own quirks, but there was no mistaking the weight of their presence. They possessed a kind of authority and power that caused others to take them seriously, trust their counsel and honor their authority. People with gravitas are more composed. They operate with personal security and gain the confidence of those they influence. Whether in movies, books, TV shows, or real life, people with gravitas are usually those we aspire to be. Why? Because we all want that type of influence.

Hold on. When was the last time someone shared their concern about not having enough gravitas with you? When was the last time you even heard this word? Why has this word fallen out of popular use? Today, if you do a Google search, you will find a

---

3 https://en.m.wikipedia.org/wiki/Gravitas

4 http://self-expression.com/speaking-freely/obstacles-to-exuding-gravitas-leadership-presence/

few articles about the importance of gravitas for corporate executives, but why not for everyone else? What about moms, dads, friends, or middle managers? Shouldn't we all want gravitas?

I think we have learned to associate gravitas with royalty or those movers and shakers we see in the news. But I assure you, every person needs gravitas to have sustainable influence. The people we have most respected in our lives, those leaders we have most admired, have gravitas. Some mistake gravitas for the X-factor that separates leaders from non-leaders, but one thing I can assure you, significant influence in any area of our lives requires gravitas.

> Significant influence in any area of our lives requires *gravitas.*

I define gravitas as having the qualities that cause others to respect us, trust us, and want to follow us. Who doesn't want that? This desire for gravitas and influence is so wired into our humanity that we see small children jockeying for control over what game is played among their friends. They fight over who gets to sit next to whom at lunch. We see teens become consumed by how many followers they have on social media or how many likes their posts receive. As human beings, we are designed to be influenced and to have influence.

Of course, some have abused their gravitas. They have led others astray, taken advantage of the weak, and have led nations into unthinkable atrocities. But this is no reason to fear gravitas. Instead, we need more people who pursue gravitas for the sake of making the world a better place. Gravitas is a quality we can all acquire to help us and others accomplish goals, pursue passions, and realize dreams. Developing gravitas is what turns us into movers and shakers in the parts of the world we inhabit.

Leadership gravitas is a phrase I use to describe my lifelong journey of integrating my desire for influence with a responsibility to influence for good. There are many leadership skills I have learned and recommend. Still, leadership gravitas goes deeper into the character of a leader. Most of us can operate well when life is going our way, but what happens to us when the pressure is on? It's in the trenches of life that our true character is revealed. This is where we discover whether we have leadership gravitas, whether we have the internal fortitude and staying power to operate well even when those around us are faltering.

Developing my own leadership gravitas has transformed every area of my life and leadership for the better. It has made me someone others respect, trust and follow more easily. Leadership gravitas dramatically increased my ability to lead and influence others. I've learned to leverage all my resources for what's in the best interest of those I lead. I have learned leadership gravitas is not selfish or self-aggrandizing. It does not pursue my good at the expense of others. It is not arrogant or egotistical. It is not insecure, petty, or self-promoting. Leadership gravitas is the freedom to operate as the best version of ourselves. Leadership gravitas is for everyone and benefits everyone.

> *Leadership gravitas* is for everyone and benefits everyone.

IMPOSTER SYNDROME

Over the past few years, I have worked with an increasing number of leaders who suffer from imposter syndrome. Imposter syndrome is a debilitating condition of mind and emotion stemming from a doubting of one's own competencies and skills. We find it difficult to accept our achievements or attribute our success to factors other than our own leadership. People who suffer from imposter syndrome describe feeling like a fraud, that they're waiting to be found out, or that it's only a matter of time before others discover they don't have what it takes. They often feel inadequate for the task at hand.

If imposter syndrome isn't addressed, we begin to believe we're not leaders after all. Perhaps we weren't born with the leadership gene. Perhaps we're not smart enough, or charismatic enough or strong enough. Perhaps we're too old, too young, or too undereducated. We imposters should settle for less. Let me tell you—these are lies.

If insecurity, fear, and self-doubt are the ailments of imposter syndrome, then anxiety, constant second-guessing, and paralysis are its symptoms. What is our antidote? Developing our leadership gravitas.

All of us suffer from imposter syndrome to some extent. We all deal with insecurities and self-doubt. The solution is not to fake it until we make it. Pretending confidence serves us no better than the emperor who paraded through his kingdom completely naked in Hans Christian Andersen's folktale, "The Emperor's New Clothes." The king convinced himself he was wearing clothes when in fact, he was not. He was delusional. We need something more than self-deceptive pretending. We need to be clothed in real confidence.

But, where does real confidence come from?

People who have leadership gravitas have confidence. Their confidence is not in a tale they tell themselves. It is a sober and accurate understanding of who they are, what they have to offer, and the value they bring to any situation. Confidence is born from this kind of personal clarity. Insecurity is born from a distorted self-perception. To put it simply, sober clarity breeds authentic confidence. This is a hallmark trait of those who are developing their leadership gravitas.

This book is an invitation to let go of the facade and step into greater clarity of who you are and the incredible influence you are meant to enjoy. You will discover yourself in a new light and learn to accept your best qualities and accept your worst. You will develop a weightier character, the kind that can move the world rather than being easily moved by the world. You will have the opportunity to exchange your insecurities and self-doubt for a wardrobe of sober self-assessment and a renewed belief that you too can live and lead with increased clarity, confidence, and courage.

ANOTHER POWERFUL TRUTH

Here's another truth no one told me. *You can only lead others to the degree that you can lead yourself.*

A recent study on the qualities of the most successful fortune 500 CEOs revealed that the number one determiner of their success was self-awareness.[5] And self-awareness, as we'll discover together, is the beginning of self-leadership. So why are these high-level executives so deeply concerned about leading themselves? Because our ability to lead others is directly and proportionately related to how well we can lead ourselves. In other words, *we can only give to others what we have first cultivated within ourselves.* There is no escaping this reality.

Interestingly, the idea of self-leadership has been largely overlooked. Most leadership resources focus on how to manage, inspire, motivate and influence other people. These are important skills, but these resources are largely others-focused. Why are there not more books or conferences inviting us to take a long, hard look into what's happening inside ourselves? I would ask you to consider this, I think we overlook self-leadership because we all share a fear of what we'll find. Often, it's just easier to focus on others and neglect our own developmental journey. But like I said, we can't help others until we've helped ourselves.

Leadership gravitas focuses first on how to lead yourself—because a leader who leads him or herself will influence others with greater ease.

5 https://www.forbes.com/sites/victorlipman/2013/11/18/all-successful-leaders-need-this-quality-Self-Awareness/?sh=6ef4386e1f06

Leadership gravitas focuses first on how to lead yourself— because a leader who leads him or herself will influence others with greater ease.

By the time I hit my early thirties I had consumed about every leadership resource within my reach and still found myself deeply frustrated by my lack of growth. Even with all the information I had acquired, all it took was a bit of pressure to expose my insecurities and inadequacies. I had plenty of leadership opportunities but no gravitas. I had many great leadership ideas but no muscle to make them work when the going got tough.

This book is an invitation to establish within yourself a quality of leadership character and capacity that will give you all the power you need to practice effective leadership across every area of your life. I am not offering tips, tricks, or one-off ideas. I am not offering solutions to specific leadership challenges. Instead, I am offering you an opportunity to develop a leadership engine that will empower your best leadership in any situation.

YOU ARE A LEADER

I wrote this book believing *everyone is a leader*. If you have any influence in the world, you are a leader. First, we are leaders of ourselves, then we are leaders of others. Regardless of your job, your industry, or your age, the world needs the best version of your leadership. *You* are a leader. Leadership isn't a hat you put on or take off, and it isn't associated with a particular title. It's who we were all born to be. Leadership is required for every human engagement. To influence or affect others is to lead them. The question is not whether we are leaders, but how intentional we are about our leadership.

Let me say it again—YOU ARE A LEADER.

Developing your leadership gravitas will mean you can access an internal strength, maturity, and wisdom most others struggle to find. This doesn't mean you'll have all the answers or always know what to do, but you will become the best at understanding your situation and yourself. You'll have the emotional wherewithal to lead with clarity and confidence in the face of the unknown. This is great leadership. This is what I'm inviting you into.

In my journey to becoming a great leader, I discovered an uncomfortable reality; *I am my own worst enemy.* It sucks, but it's true. I am the reason I get stuck and plateau. It took me a long time to realize I preferred blaming everyone around me for my failures. But the hard truth about myself and every leader I've worked with is this: until we take 100% responsibility for our journey, success will elude us. Personal responsibility is a terrible-tasting medicine, but without it, we cannot elevate to the quality of life and leadership we aspire to. As long as we blame others for why we are where we are, as long as we play the victim, great leadership is out of reach.

Taking personal responsibility only tastes horrible because it exposes the dysfunctions of our character and ability. I'm not saying life isn't full of unfortunate, frustrating, and unfair experiences. Thankfully, our future does not have to be defined by them. We have the power to determine our future by the way we respond to life's challenges. The stories we tell ourselves and the meaning we assign to our experiences will determine our attitudes and behaviors. And our behaviors shape our lives.

This is why we love movies in which the main character overcomes incredible challenges, even ones they did not invite, to attain breakthroughs and achieve great things. We all want that story. You and I are hardwired to grow and to do great things. Our passage of freedom into this desirable future rests not on fate, our family, our opportunities, or what school we went to, but on our willingness to accept the challenge of personal transformation. Our future depends on the kind of people we are becoming.

I know the frustration of plateauing, struggling through transition, suffering dysfunctions, and failing to operate well within teams and organizations. My team and I have helped thousands of leaders overcome these barriers. We've done the same in our own lives as well. We've spent years learning the secret to negotiating and overcoming these challenges in any context. So, what is the secret to developing our leadership gravitas? *Becoming emotionally intelligent leaders!*

Emotional intelligence (EQ) is the skill set we need to cultivate our weightiness. EQ is the internal engine that will unlock the best version of ourselves for every situation we encounter. Over the years, I have discovered emotional intelligence is the greatest determining factor of great leadership. This is the competitive advantage we're all looking for.

HOW WE GET THERE

This book is framed by a simple tool I call the Emotional Intelligence Matrix (EQ Matrix for short). The EQ Matrix is a simple framework outlining the key pathway and skills we'll need to grow our leadership gravitas. These skills are deeply rooted in my understanding of emotional intelligence. Emotional intelligence is simply understood as an ability to practice awareness and leadership of both ourselves and others. The good news is this: these skills can be applied to every relationship in your life, thereby making the contents of this book incredibly valuable (of course, I'm a bit biased). We'll learn how to practice personal responsibility, lead ourselves with greater awareness, and lead others, so they want to follow. This is the pathway to influence!

My intention here is to bridge the gap from the academic conversation to the everyday practice of emotional intelligence for success in every area of life. I am a committed EQ practitioner, and I speak out of the overflow of my own journey. My personal story will serve as the laboratory in which together we discover a better pathway. Leaders need more than good ideas and expert theories. We need more than tips and techniques. We need a way forward that transcends textbook leadership. *Leadership Gravitas* will show you this pathway along with the practical skills to make emotionally intelligent leadership part of your everyday life.

Simply put, the leaders who walk this pathway become a better version of themselves.

I have two main goals with this book. My first goal is to define personal responsibility and show why it's more powerful than any other leadership approach. The second goal is to provide a reliable tool you can use in any leadership situation. As you learn to employ the Emotional Intelligence Matrix in your everyday life, your gravitas will increase, leadership becomes second nature, and people follow happily.

I have identified three core skills for each of the four quadrants of the EQ Matrix. I'll unpack those skills for you, quadrant by quadrant, as we learn to practice the Pathway of Personal Responsibility. Each skill will offer you an opportunity to reflect diagnostically on your own leadership capacity along with practical handles to develop each one.

FINALLY

In our best moments, we all practice a fair amount of emotional intelligence. The problem we run into is that we're not always sure how we did it, which makes it difficult to repeat, especially under pressure. The EQ Matrix and the practical applications offered in the chapters ahead are meant to fix that problem. This tool gives us practical handles to intentionalize what before was floating around in our subconscious. From there, EQ becomes a proactive habit, part of who we are.

In the chapters ahead, I will share some of the most important lessons I've learned about emotional intelligence, taking 100% responsibility for who I am, how I engage life, and how I lead myself and others. I have written from the overflow of my own story, hoping somewhere in the messiness of my journey, you will find hope and direction for yours.

My mission here is simple: your transformation. I invite you to join me on this journey toward more personal power and influence. The choice is yours!

02
THE POWER OF CHOICE

"You may have just sunk our company!" The words hit me like a Conor McGregor punch to the solar plexus. I could hardly breathe. My boss and mentor had called me into his office to inform me that I had just driven away our largest, most profitable client to date. How could this be? My heart raced, and my sight narrowed as the blood drained from my head. Failure had cornered me again as I felt the weight of the situation begin to press upon me. What would I do? Where could I hide? Shame crept in and left me with a deep, sinking feeling in my gut.

I knew my response to this moment would determine a lot about my future. I'm not just talking about my career being at stake, but also the kind of person I would become. I knew how I responded would reveal who I had become as a leader. But at that moment, I was overwhelmed with the shear gravity of my boss' words. How would I deal with another failure? How would I deal with that kind of exposure? How far back would it set me? Would I ever recover? What would people think of me?

Can you relate? When you look back on the life you've lived

so far, can you think of a time, a moment, or a season in which you knew your trajectory would change for better or worse? And it all hinged on your response.

My boss stared at me intently, waiting to see what I would do. I had heard him say a hundred times, "The real failure in life is failing to learn from our failures." I had a choice to make. What would I say or do? Whatever my response, it would be the beginning of a journey, not the kind of journey you look forward to, but an important one nonetheless. This was the journey of becoming the kind of leader who could shoulder all that I wanted to fight for in life—all of who I wanted to become in realizing my full potential.

Failure is a part of this journey, even though I had tried to avoid it at all costs. For me, failure was tied to my personal value. If I failed at anything, I took it to mean I was not valuable. So, I would circumvent failure by a variety of tactics. One was to project the responsibility onto someone else or an outside circumstance. Or I would attempt to simply scoot it under the rug. I would pretend like it wasn't a big deal, so it wasn't actually a failure. I would try to rationalize and justify it or try to explain it away as something unavoidable. And if none of these worked, I would actually go into full self-condemnation and self-flagellation mode. Obviously not powerful leadership qualities.

I stood stunned in front of my boss, hoping it was all just a nightmare, unable to fully process what he had just said to me. The room around me faded into obscurity, and it felt as if time was passing in slow motion. My brain felt foggy as I searched for the "right" thing to say. He was still waiting.

His words, "You may have just sunk our company," played over and over in my mind.

After what seemed an eternity, I responded how I think most of us do when we're on the defensive. I blamed the client. I was the head coach and the best our firm had. I had trained our coaches on how to coach. It was my playbook they were running day in and day out, coaching hundreds of leaders across the world. So, the failure couldn't be mine, right? It must be that the clients are un-coachable!

I had been tasked with coaching the executive team of a large organization. I explained to my boss how difficult *they* were, *their* adolescent behaviors, and how *they* rarely did their homework. I had given them three months of my time and energy with seemingly little return on my investment. How could they be unhappy with me? They deserved whatever challenge I gave them. As a matter of fact, they should be thanking me for being so patient! I was clear in my defense that *they* were the problem—not me.

I was sure I had convinced my boss the problem was all theirs. Surely, he had my back. It turns out he did, just not the way I expected. He leaned forward, removed his glasses in the way only a father figure could, and uttered, "The problem isn't that they're un-coachable, it's that you are unable to coach them."

Another gut punch! It was all I could do not to break down in tears or find or find a dark hole to hide in. My brain went into overload as I tried to make sense of what he was saying. *Was this really all my fault?* I'm sure I hadn't handled them perfectly but I was unable to comprehend how this failed relationship rested on my shoulders alone.

After exhausting every attempt to shift the responsibility back to the client, I finally surrendered to the fact there were only two options in front of me. I would either embrace my mentor's challenge or explore more excuses. I would either take personal responsibility for this failure or continue the blame game.

I had spent much of my life to this point convinced my greatest problems were someone else's fault. If everyone else could simply change, then my life would be better. This strategy had allowed me to bully my way through many relationships. But there was a new leadership threshold before me, and old strategies would have to be abandoned for new ones. If I didn't change, I would plateau, or worse, I would continue to fail.

I had sacrificed so much to move my family across the country to be mentored by the kind of leader I wanted to become, one who could be entrusted with greater responsibility. This was my opportunity to rise up and step into the role I felt called to—staring me right in the face.

He continued to stare at me. He would not let me wriggle out of this one. I felt like Frodo Baggins hearing that I was the one who had to undertake the terrible journey to destroy the ring in the fires of Mount Doom in Mordor. I had to make a choice.

This wasn't the first time my boss had shone a light on one of my leadership blind spots. He had been training me in the business of taking personal responsibility, which he believed was a key ingredient to leadership growth. He knew it would make or break my long-term success as a leader across every area of my life. I knew deep down that blaming others wouldn't actually solve the problem, even if it did make me feel better momentarily.

I knew deep down that *blaming others wouldn't actually solve the problem,* even if it did make me feel better momentarily.

I took a deep breath, then I took an even bigger risk. I chose to take personal responsibility, which meant I would have to take a good, hard look at myself. I would have to see things I really didn't want to see about myself. I would have to embrace my own need for change if I hoped to be a change agent for other leaders. As they say in the South (we were in South Carolina after all), I would have to eat humble pie.

If I had found an easier way, I would gladly share it with you. My journey wasn't easy, but the value it has brought to my life and to so many others demands that I make it available for anyone daring enough to stare themselves in the face, recognize where they need to grow, and fight for a better version of themselves. Is that you? If so, you're in the right place.

LEADERSHIP GRAVITAS

The phrase "leadership gravitas" came to me through a variety of conversations with several people, but mainly it arose out of an illustration of the gravitational pull of planetary orbits. To put it simply, bodies of lesser mass orbit around bodies of larger mass. To become a leader that other people can safely orbit around, we must increase our leadership mass—our character, integrity, trustworthiness, and stability. Self-awareness and self-leadership are at the heart of cultivating our leadership gravitas. Without these characteristics, we become unpredictable and unsafe for the people we intend to lead. We might overreact. We might withdraw. Passive-aggressive comments might suddenly come out. And so, because of our lack of predictability, people feel unsafe and tend to shrink back from us. It makes it difficult for people to want to follow us. Leadership gravitas is about cultivating that internal leadership integrity via self-awareness and self-leadership. That means other people can safely orbit around us without being injured or frightened.

I have found that practicing the Pathway of Personal Responsibility (which I will discuss later in this book) has a radically transforming effect on myself and people I have coached. As we increase our self-awareness and cultivate self-leadership, we find our center, feel more secure, and operate with greater poise. Practicing self-leadership increases our leadership gravitas. We no longer feel the need to control the world around us because we're finally in control of ourselves.

Increasing my own leadership gravitas has transformed how I lead in every situation. I am less reactive with my wife and

Practicing self-leadership increases our leadership gravitas. We no longer feel the need to control the world around us because we're finally in control of ourselves.

kids. They can count on me to listen before I speak. They trust I am interested in their perspectives and opinions. We may not always agree, but they know we will work together to discover the best solutions. Those on my team have confidence that I have their best interest in mind when processing problems and making decisions. They know I believe in them and will fight to help them increase their own leadership gravitas, rise through the ranks and become the best version of themselves.

Our clients have dubbed us "business therapists" because we not only help them transform their business culture, we help them transform their personal culture. They trust they are more than a paycheck. We will leverage everything at our disposal to help them become the best version of themselves to create the most powerful leadership cultures in the world.

Self-awareness and self-leadership are the most sought-after skills by top executives in the world. Why? Because there is a simple principle that serves as the foundation for every expression of great leadership. It is deeply rooted in our understanding of emotional intelligence. *You can only lead others to the degree that you lead yourself.* Our educational systems offered little to no attention to these skills and many of us received less in our childhood homes. For me, learning to lead myself is a lifelong commitment. For the sake of my family and businesses, may there never be a day when I convince myself that I have arrived and no longer need personal transformation.

I started this book with a story of my own failure to show you that no matter how broken you may feel or how stuck you may be, the choice to grow, to transform, to become a better version of yourself, is always at your fingertips. No one else can do it for you. It's your choice. You have to put in the hard work. Perhaps the greatest power any human has is the power of choice. We cannot control the world around us, but we can choose how we respond and shape our environment. Every day, every moment is an opportunity to exercise your power. You get to choose. Even continuing to read this book is your choice. One thing I can tell you, the journey isn't always going to be easy, but it is well worth it!

*You can only lead others to the degree that **you lead yourself.***

03

TRIGGERS, HIJACKING &
PINBALLING

As a child, I loved playing the pinball machines at the local arcade. Yes, I know I'm dating myself, but the metaphor nicely explains a familiar experience in life. We drop a couple quarters into the slot, launch the steel ball into the heart of the machine, and watch as it bounces uncontrollably off the various triggers. As the player, we are tasked with keeping the ball out of the gutter using flippers and a lot of luck. Lose focus for even a moment, and your ball will inevitably be swallowed up in the gutter. The experience of playing a pinball machine was exhilarating to say the least. But it also left me feeling stressed and frantic.

Ever feel like you're the little steel ball in a pinball machine, thrust into the moment-by-moment triggers of life? Bouncing off the walls, desperately trying to stay out of the gutter? Too often, it seems as if life is batting us around, sending us in uncontrollable directions, and causing us to behave in erratic ways.

From the moment we wake up until we go to bed, we're assaulted by life's triggers. Positive ones, negative ones, confusing ones, big ones, little ones. Your alarm blares at you well before you're ready to get out of bed. Now you've snoozed so many times you're running late. A quick check of your texts or emails reveals more problems at work. Your roommate or significant other used the last coffee pod, so now you have to run through Starbucks—but you're already late! Some jerk cuts you off on the freeway, you hit every red light and the city planner decided today is the day to do road work, so you now have orange-barrel delays. You can't even reach your desk without remembering the project that's running behind, the high maintenance client who is awaiting your call back, and the coworker who greets you with a diplomatic smile hiding her ill intentions. And all of this before 9:00 a.m.!

We know these triggers by the impact they have on our thoughts, emotions, and behaviors. Our emotions are trustworthy indicators that we've been triggered. The more intense the trigger, the greater our emotional response. Negative triggers bait us to become reactive before we've had a chance to process what's happening, how we're being affected, and the best course of action.

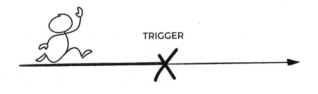

Figure 1

As largely functional humans, we're able to navigate the minefield of triggers with some decency, usually. Still, we all know it's only a matter of time before one big trigger or lots of little ones compound and put us on tilt. Most days, we're able to navigate the trigger minefield without having a blow-up. But as the pressures of life mount, it's easy to lose it and get derailed. Because the human brain is lightning fast—faster than a thousand super computers—our brain assesses these triggers, chooses the quickest and easiest pathway for survival, then calls our body (or our mouth) into reactive behaviors. BAM! We're hijacked!

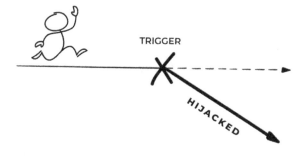

Figure 2

Being hijacked is what happens when the worst version of ourselves jumps into the driver's seat. We find ourselves reacting impulsively as if our anger, frustration, impatience, passivity, or withdrawal are the only pathways to regain control or safety. The more triggered we are, the more feverishly we fight to hold things together. But everyone—and I mean every single human on earth—has a breaking point. When sufficiently triggered, we lose our composure and say or do something stupid. We've been hijacked.

As Figure 2 reveals, when hijacked, the trajectory of our lives changes. This happens whether we want it to or not. We can pretend that we're still traveling the dotted line, but this becomes a form of self-delusion and denial. It's our inability to recognize that our trajectory has shifted that gets us in so much trouble. Failing to recognize that we've been hijacked means we're running blind. Have you ever run through your house at night without any lights on? When sufficiently hijacked, the insecure, fearful, and self-protecting part of ourselves takes over, and the pinballing has begun!

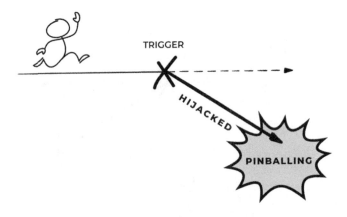

Figure 3

Pinballing is a phrase we use to describe when life feels out of control. We can pinball for minutes, days, or even months on end. Triggers lead to a hijacking, and if we're not equipped to recover quickly enough, we will find ourselves pinballing. I have watched as close friends pinballed through most of the recent presidential election. As humans, we're wired to handle short bursts of stress and anxiety, but pinballing is when this becomes our way of life. There's just no way to operate as the best version of ourselves in this condition. We need a way out. We need a way to recover ourselves and regain our internal compass.

I'M A RECOVERING PINBALLER

Sometimes a single trigger is all it takes to send us into chaos—a comment from a friend or a questionable look from our spouse. Unfinished dishes in the sink have caused me to fly off the handle. Unexpected traffic has solicited rage behaviors on the freeway, and stubbing my toe on the corner of my bed can put me in a terrible mood for the rest of the day. No matter your title, role, responsibility, age, or season of life, we all get triggered and hijacked.

I was definitely triggered repeatedly by the behaviors of the executive team I was working with. In the early coaching sessions, I was able to maintain my composure and stay the course. This wasn't my first rodeo. But unresolved triggers have a way of compounding stress and frustration. My impatience grew. The more I was triggered, the more I sought to control the environment. I thought I knew better, but after some time, I was hijacked, then pinballing through each session. I became increasingly reactive and even surprised myself with passive-aggressive behaviors.

The problem is that most of us aren't even aware we're pinballing until the consequences are louder than our internal chaos. And often times it's too late. The damage has been done. Trust has been broken. Relationships are fractured. Promotions are lost. Clients stop returning. Significant others withdraw. Children cower in fear or feel ignored.

If we're not careful, pinballing can easily become a lifestyle of semi-controlled chaos. We blame everyone and everything else for why we're so angry, sad, frustrated, unhappy, unfulfilled, or unlucky. We take on a helpless-hopeless victim mentality. We convince ourselves that life is happening to us, and we believe there is nothing we can do about it. This puts us in a reactive, defensive posture. We get stuck and find our relationships, leadership, and careers plateauing—or plummeting. We need a game plan. We need a way to flip the script on the pinballing experience that puts the best version of ourselves back in the driver's seat.

> We need a way to flip the script on the pinballing experience that puts the best version of ourselves back in the driver's seat.

When was the last time you blew up on a coworker or your spouse, but you knew your reaction had little or nothing to do with that person? That's pinballing. Have you ever made rash decisions you later realized were born out of impatience or frustration? That's pinballing. Are there people in your life you avoid or treat poorly on account of unresolved issues? That's pinballing. Have you ever given another driver the one-finger salute because they cut you off? That's pinballing. Have you yelled at your kids because they were having fun but making too much noise? That's pinballing. Have you walked away from a meeting, client, or conversation because you were fed up with the nonsense? That's pinballing.

Here's the good news...*It doesn't have to be that way!* And guess what? *You're not alone, either!* The most successful people get triggered, hijacked, and even pinball at times. To be triggered is to be human. Our leadership gravitas is not determined by whether we get triggered, but how we respond to those triggers.

Here's even more good news. I am going to give you some tools and help you develop skills to identify your triggers and understand the impact they have on your life and your behaviors. I will show you an alternative pathway that will give you confidence and enable you to handle the hijackings that are certainly coming your way. As a leader, you need to be ready to operate with clarity, confidence, and courage amidst the increasing pressures of life and leadership. And I'm here to help you do just that.

THE GAME PLAN: AN ALTERNATIVE PATHWAY

As we travel through life and encounter triggers, it often seems there is only one way to respond. I call these our default behaviors because we fall back on them unconsciously. We get triggered and react almost impulsively to self-protect, deflect, or overpower a situation. Someone says something we disagree with, so we put on our boxing gloves and prepare for a fight. We didn't land the potential client, and we blame them for why it didn't work. Our boss barks at us during a meeting, so we withdraw and refuse to engage any longer. The corporate decision doesn't go our way, so we sulk and seek to sabotage its future. The table below gives us a quick blink at how triggers correspond with default behaviors.

TRIGGER	DEFAULT BEHAVIOR
Someone says something we disagree with	Put our boxing gloves on and prepare for a fight
We didn't land the potential client	We blame them for why it didn't work
Our boss barks at us during a meeting	We withdraw and refuse to engage any longer
The corporate decision didn't go our way	We sulk and seek to sabotage its future

Table 1

The predicament we all face every time we're triggered is a potential hijacking. When we are hijacked, we find ourselves responding with default behaviors. These default behaviors often become predictable and consistent, creating a well-worn pathway. I call it our default pathway (Figure 4). Even though most of us would admit to the painful and destructive nature of our negative default behaviors and pathways, we don't know another option. Of course, we all tell ourselves we won't react the same way next time. We'll have more self-control. We won't yell or we won't cower. But when we encounter a similar trigger, it's almost inevitable that we'll be well down the default pathway before we know what's happened.

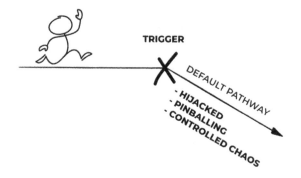

Figure 4

If it looks like your default behaviors can send you over a cliff, that's because they can. Or at least they'll take you downhill as opposed to raising your confidence and credibility as a leader.

Spend enough time with someone else and you can begin to predict their responses to different situations. Growing up, I could predict that my father would yell at me and my brothers if we disturbed his peace in any way. I could predict my mother would do her best to protect us from his wrath. I could predict the fight they would get in as they battled for parental supremacy. I could predict that if a bully pushed my older brother too far, he would land his fist square on the bully's nose. If my younger brother was threatened, I could predict that he would retreat into isolation. These are default behaviors. Not all default behaviors are necessarily bad, but as leaders, we must become more acquainted with our own and their impact on our decisions.

These default behaviors wired into our brains are often learned from our earliest years. They are *the way* we're conditioned to respond to triggers without even thinking about it. For example, if you had an older sibling who picked on you as a child, you may have learned to lash out at anyone you perceive to be taunting or criticizing you. Or if you had a parent who got angry anytime you were noisy, you may have learned to shut down, stop talking, or walk away when someone confronts you.

These conditioned responses have developed over the years through various encounters in which we have learned to "fight, fly, or fold." The problem is that we fly through life and into these default behaviors and their inevitable consequences without realizing there is an alternative pathway. They are so automatic that we rarely have control over them—until we recondition ourselves and increase our emotional intelligence. And that is what we'll address as we unpack the EQ Matrix.

Increasing our leadership gravitas demands that we become aware of our negative default behaviors—the ones that get us in trouble and do not offer the best version of ourselves to the situation. But we must also learn to identify the triggers that sent us coursing into self-sabotage in the first place. We must recognize there is a fork in the road at every trigger! Remember, we all get triggered. And every trigger is an opportunity to choose a preferred pathway of behavior that reflects composure, clarity, and confidence. Great leaders learn the skills for recognizing and transforming every trigger into a growth opportunity.

> *Great leaders* learn the skills for recognizing and transforming every trigger into a growth opportunity.

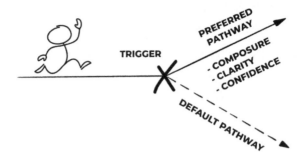

Figure 5

We all want to be the best version of ourselves more often. By learning to identify and process the triggers we experience, we'll be better positioned to decide which pathway to choose. Instead of picking up the broken pieces that result from our unhealthy default behaviors, we will learn preferred behaviors that will yield better outcomes for everyone involved. Eventually, the preferred pathway becomes our new default pathway.

What kind of circumstances or people trigger you most? Can you predict your own responses to various triggers? Keep those in mind as we turn our attention now to the tool and process that will help you identify your triggers, choose an alternative pathway, and operate proactively with the best version of yourself. Now, who doesn't want that?

EMOTIONAL INTELLIGENCE AND PERSONAL RESPONSIBILITY

The simplest and most important way to increase your leadership gravitas and unlock every breakthrough you'll ever need is to develop your emotional intelligence (EQ). Daniel Goleman, in his seminal book entitled *Emotional Intelligence: Why It Can Matter More Than IQ* (1995), argues that EQ is at least as important, if not more important, than IQ (intelligence quotient) for sustainable success in any area of life. Why is this?

Emotional intelligence is "the capacity to be aware of, control, and express one's emotions, and to handle interpersonal relationships judiciously and empathetically."[6] We've all heard someone say, "It's not *what* you said, but *how* you said it." Think of it this way. The *what* is an expression of IQ. The *how* is an

---

6 https://www.google.com/search?q=google+dictionary+english&oq=google+dict&aqs=-chrome.2.0i131i433i457j69i57j0i433j0l2j0i433j0i131i433j0.5204j0j7&sourceid=chrome&ie=UTF-8#dobs=Emotional%20intelligence%20

expression of EQ. Both matter, but how often is our *what* undermined by our *how*? 90% of the arguments I have with my wife are derailed because the "brilliant" points we're trying to make are shrouded in combativeness, insensitivity, and impatience. The same goes for any environment in which people are trying to work together. Our IQ is often undermined by our lack of EQ.

> # Our IQ is often undermined by our *lack of EQ.*

I spend much of my time working with leaders, teams, and organizations in which IQ clearly isn't the problem. The truth is, you can have multiple degrees, loads of experience, and even be an industry expert but still lack the emotional intelligence to build a healthy leadership culture marked by trust, open engagement, and collaborative partnership.

I've taken the best of all I have learned after years of studying and practicing emotional intelligence and created a simple visual tool that will give you a roadmap for practicing the basic skills of emotional intelligence across every area of your life. You will learn to identify your own triggers, take stock of the impact they have on you, and learn a new pathway that promises you'll be operating with greater EQ. This chapter will introduce the roadmap and the following chapters will provide a deep dive into the core skills you can learn and practice to grow your EQ muscles.

THE EQ MATRIX

EQ helps us understand the two relationships we deal with on a regular basis—with ourselves and with others. Within those relationships, there are two primary engagements: Awareness and Leadership. When we put these on a simple matrix, we discover there are four quadrants that can help us to better understand the landscape of our lives. Every experience we have can be understood through these four quadrants, as diagrammed in Figure 6 below.

EQ MATRIX

	AWARE	LEAD
OTHERS	OTHER-AWARENESS	OTHER-LEADERSHIP
SELF	SELF-AWARENESS	SELF-LEADERSHIP

Figure 6

The top quadrants of Other-Awareness and Other-Leadership represent how we see and interact with other people and circumstances. The lower quadrants of Self-Awareness and Self-Leadership represent how we engage our own thoughts, emotions, and behaviors, which ultimately determine how we engage with the external world.

It's important to understand that our outward attitudes and behaviors are always the overflow of what's happening *inside us*, not the result of what's happening *to us*. In other words, how we behave in the upper two quadrants is always the overflow of what's happening in our inner world represented by the lower quadrants. This is why so many of us seek professional psychiatric help through counselors, psychologists, and psychiatrists. We're trying to understand the relationship between what's happening above and below the line.

EQ MATRIX

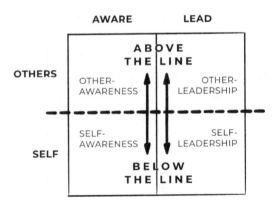

Figure 7

Here's a major part of the problem. We spend the better part of our days almost exclusively focused on what's happening above the line in the upper right quadrant of Other-Leadership. This is where the rubber meets the road in our daily life. We get triggered, hijacked, and experience pinballing in our interaction with others. Then, we spend way too much time and energy trying to navigate what happened.

You'll notice 75% of our time, energy, and resources are focused on 25% of what determines how we operate (see Figure 8). Without knowing how to navigate all four quadrants, we undoubtedly find ourselves living reactively, surviving life rather than proactively engaging it. This is why it's easier to blame everyone and everything else in our lives for how we feel, think, and behave.

TRIGGERED

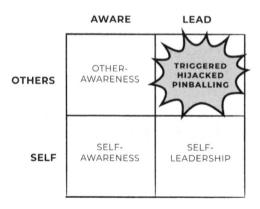

Figure 8

In learning about the fate of the Titanic, I discovered that icebergs have 90% of their mass hidden beneath the water. That means 10% is visible at best. If we're only dealing with 10% of a problem, we're only likely to find 10% of the solution. No wonder the Titanic didn't stand a chance! Like the roots of a tree, the engine of a car, and the hidden mass of an iceberg, our attitudes and behaviors are largely driven by what's happening beneath the surface of our own lives.

The degree to which we know how to engage our internal world through Self-Awareness and Self-Leadership is the degree to which we can more effectively navigate Other-Awareness and Other-Leadership. If we are not equipped to do this, we're likely to suffer the same fate as the Titanic.

As I said before, we all get triggered, even hijacked. In our worst moments, we're pinballing, but it doesn't have to stay that way. We have a choice. Will we continue to spend most of our energy trying to control what's happening in the upper right quadrant (leading others)? Or will we start paying attention to what's happening below the line (leading ourselves), so we are better prepared to engage our triggers? We can either blame the world around us for our attitudes and behaviors, or take personal responsibility.

THE PATHWAY OF PERSONAL RESPONSIBILITY

The Pathway of Personal Responsibility invites us to see every trigger as an indicator of what's happening for us internally. Our triggers serve us in the same way the needles on the dashboard of our cars let us know what's happening beneath the hood. Triggers—even as annoying and inconvenient as they seem—are gifts. Without them, we'd be flying blind! Imagine that, no instruments to tell us if our engine is running hot or whether we have enough fuel to make it to our destination. Triggers indicate that we've been disrupted and we are no longer operating from a position of clarity. A hijacking is imminent if we don't respond well.

In the story I began in Chapter 1, I was content to blame the executive team of leaders I found so difficult. I was regularly triggered and had convinced myself they were the problem. If only they would change, be coachable, then I could do my job and prove successful! I would explain to anyone who would listen why they were making my life miserable. I deemed them "un-coachable" and wrote them off. I made them wrong so I could feel right. Sadly, I didn't initially realize what a gift they were to me. I saw them as an obstacle and missed an incredible opportunity to learn from my reactions and become a better leader.

As you look back at the EQ Matrix (Figure 6), consider each trigger as an invitation to pay attention to what's happening within you. This begins by practicing Self-Awareness. You can't change what you can't see, and you don't know what you don't know. We all have blind spots that hinder our view of ourselves. Recognizing triggers and practicing Self-Awareness can help us discover what gets in our way.

Self-Awareness postures us to practice Self-Leadership. Again, we can only lead others to the degree that we can lead ourselves! Once we've dealt with what's beneath the surface, we're ready to engage the world around us with increased emotional and mental sobriety—with greater clarity, confidence, and courage. We then become "Others-Aware" and leading becomes more natural and exponentially more effective.

You can't change what you can't see, and you don't know what you don't know.

In my own journey and in my interactions with those I have coached, I have found that practicing the Pathway of Personal Responsibility has a radically transforming effect. Let's go back to the pinball illustration. Imagine the little steel ball chaotically bouncing around the table, hijacked by every new trigger. Now imagine throwing a softball into the same machine. What about a basketball? Now imagine a bowling ball!

Sure, the bowling ball will still be hit by triggers, but its mass makes it less movable. This is what happens as we learn to identify and process triggers through the Pathway of Personal Responsibility (See Figure 9). As we increase our Self-Awareness and cultivate Self-Leadership, we find our center, feel more secure, and operate with greater poise. We can't hope to live a life free from triggers, but we can learn to live a life increasingly free from the pinballing effect. Practicing EQ increases our leadership gravitas. We no longer feel the need to control the world around us because we're finally in control of ourselves. As a result, the people under our leadership feel safe and confident to orbit around us. The synergy that produces will ultimately affect our bottom line—and that's good for everyone.

PATHWAY OF PERSONAL RESPONSIBILITY

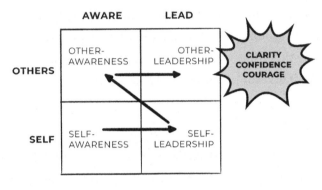

Figure 9

THE STAKES ARE HIGH

Before we jump in and learn the Pathway of Personal Responsibility skills, let me make something very clear. In friendship, family, business, or any other grand endeavor, partnerships with other people are our greatest asset. They are non-negotiable. And these relationships rise and fall to the degree that emotional intelligence is understood and practiced.

Emotional intelligence is the leadership engine that will power our greatest passions and dreams. This system enables us to work collaboratively with others to accomplish so much more than we could on our own. In the words of an African proverb, *"If you want to go fast, go alone, but if you want to go far, go together."* Human beings are tribal creatures. No matter how difficult it can be to do, we find ourselves undeniably drawn to link arms and partner with others. Together, we can count the cost, clarify our mission, and call ourselves a team. We become an expression of what all human beings have longed for throughout history—a team on a mission. We can call ourselves a family, a tribe, a nation, a company, a team, a division, or a squad. Any way you look at it, we're fighting for the same thing—to join a team and battle for a common mission.

Think about it. We're all born into a family. For many of us, that becomes our team for the next couple of decades. This is where we develop our identity, discover our unique talents and contributions, and shape our character and core values. When we leave home, some of us head off to college, where we immediately seek a new family or team to join. Whether it's a fraternity, sorority, or special interest club, we're looking for others with whom we share a common affinity or activity. We're looking to join a family/team on a mission.

Falling in love with my wife and having children was just us doing what humans love to do—building a family on a mission. Starting multiple businesses over the years was just my wife and I doing what we're wired to do—building teams on a mission. In the same way Other-Leadership doesn't seem to work without the foundation of Self-Leadership, the missions we're passionate to engage don't work well without a family (or team) prepared to live and die for one another...at least figuratively speaking.

When it comes to building a team on a mission, learning the Pathway of Personal Responsibility, increasing our emotional intelligence, and leading ourselves is paramount to leading others. Like I said, *the stakes are incredibly high!* I have staked my entire life and leadership on this conversation and the discoveries we will go on to explore together. The stakes are too high not to give ourselves completely to this journey.

Before we jump in to learn the practical skills for practicing EQ, I encourage you to take a moment and reflect on a few questions:

- What are the most important missions in my life currently?

- Who are the families, tribes, or teams that are essential to accomplish our missions?

- On a scale of 1-10, how effectively are those teams operating?

- On a scale of 1-10, how well do I contribute to the overall success of these teams?

No matter how you answered those questions, your tribe needs your leadership. Furthermore, the world needs the *best version of your leadership!* Now, let's jump in and build our EQ muscles!

QUADRANT 1:
SELF-AWARENESS

Our journey on the Pathway of Personal Responsibility begins with Self-Awareness. Remember, every trigger, hijacking, or pinballing experience is an opportunity to look inside ourselves, beginning with Self-Awareness. Our ability to practice the other quadrants largely depends on how well we're practicing this quadrant. Self-Awareness is the foundation for emotional intelligence. If the foundation is good, then we can build confidently upon it. A faulty foundation will reveal itself later in unwanted patterns of attitudes and behaviors. When someone diagnoses a problem in one of the other three quadrants, the problem often lies somewhere in Self-Awareness.

SELF-AWARENESS

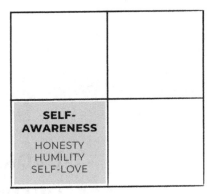

Figure 10

Self-Awareness is a "conscious knowledge of one's own character, feelings, motives and desires."[7] The word *conscious* suggests we have to bring it out of the darkness into the light, out of

---

7 Oxford American College Dictionary

the unseen realm into the seen. The journey into Self-Awareness requires courage, vulnerability, and hope as we're sure to meet with things we'd rather ignore than see.

Thankfully Self-Awareness is a skill anyone can learn and practice regularly. Developing this skill is the key that unlocks the change of trajectory in our life and leadership. As we become more aware of what is going on inside us, we can better engage and traverse the world around us.

The three core skills for practicing Self-Awareness are honesty, humility, and self-love. We'll unpack those one at a time in the next three chapters.

HONESTY

S hell-shocked by the news that I had possibly sunk our company with my mentor awaiting my response, I had a choice to make. Would I a) continue to blame and deflect my failure on others or, b) have the courage to practice brutal honesty with myself? At that moment, option "a" felt much better to me. But I had known my mentor enough to recognize he was giving me an *opportunity to choose*. Honesty or self-preservation. Which would it be?

Honesty shines a light into the darkness, like an X-ray or MRI of our body, or the scale we stand on in our bathroom. The true nature of honesty is often misunderstood. Honesty has no moral compass, no agenda, no values to promote other than itself. Honesty is not our judge or jury. It simply exposes *what is*—with no reasons or excuses. Honesty cares about facts, not opinions. And without the facts we're destined to develop distorted opinions.

We define honesty in EQ as the accurate assessment of our thoughts, attitudes, and behaviors along with how they impact our environment. This way of approaching honesty ensures we are practicing personal responsibility not only for what's happening inside us, but also how we affect others. In our pursuit of self-honesty, we can never afford to forget this connection between our inner life and outer life.

Honesty cares about facts, not opinions. And without the facts we're destined to develop distorted opinions.

BLIND SPOTS

We call honesty a skill because we all have areas in our lives we cannot see, often known as *blind spots*. When my boss told me I was the issue in the equation, he was making me aware that I had a blind spot—something in my life I could not see accurately. Right then, I learned a simple truth: *you can't see what you can't see*, and *you don't know what you don't know*. By helping me see something I could not see before, he gave me an incredible opportunity to develop a more sober assessment of myself.

It is very difficult to practice honesty in isolation. We need trusted people in our lives who can serve as mirrors to help us increase our Self-Awareness. This can feel threatening as the lesser parts of ourselves come into view. Our pride, a.k.a. ego, will inevitably seek to protect us from exposure. But that leads us to another simple truth: *you can't change what you can't see.*

I experience this every time I visit the dentist or my auto mechanic. I go in hoping everything will be fine, but I know deep down they may expose a problem I'd rather not have to deal with. I have to trust they have my best interest in mind (this is why a trusted mechanic is so valuable), and they are seeking to help me rather than harm me. And if you're like me, you might wait until the problem has become so obvious that you have no choice. Many of us wait until our car is sputtering along on the brink of breakdown or the toothache becomes unbearable. Just as we need dentists and auto mechanics, we need trusted friends who can help us diagnose the problems in our attitudes and behaviors before they become worse and the cost goes way up!

"*BREAUTIFUL* HONESTY"

Practicing honesty can be a *"breautiful"* (brutal + beautiful) activity. I've never met anyone who enjoys having their shortcomings, inadequacies, or failures exposed. Just ask Adam and Eve!
This ancient Biblical story tells us they were made by God and
put in a heavenly garden to enjoy their friendship with God,
each other, and the work God had given them. They lived in what
some call "heaven on earth," the Garden of Eden. The story tells
us they were "naked and unashamed."[8] Nothing to hide. Fully
seen. Fully known. That is until something changed.

Adam and Eve blew it. They dropped the ball. They were triggered by the deceitful voice of a serpent who convinced them
they could not trust God and needed to take matters into their
own hands. In the same way my mentor sought me out to confront me, this ancient story tells us God did the same. "Where
are you?" God called out for them.

When they finally showed themselves, they were hiding behind leaves. When asked about what happened, Adam blamed
Eve. Eve blamed the serpent. Neither of them took personal
responsibility for their actions, choosing instead to point the
finger at everyone else. They were now "clothed and ashamed."
We often clothe ourselves with reasons and excuses for fear of
being exposed, and we blame others for our decisions, actions,
and shortcomings.

This is a *breautiful* story. It captures what I believe all humans long for—to be seen and known and have nothing to hide

---

8 Genesis 2:25

from. The problem is, like Adam and Eve, we get triggered, hijacked. and behave in ways that betray the trust of others. We fail. We blow it. We act inconsiderately, say hurtful things, lose our patience, tell lies, and act selfishly.

But what happens when we're confronted?

If Honesty is the beginning of the Pathway to Personal Responsibility, fear is the gate that blocks the path. Fear is our response to the "what ifs" of an unknown future. What if I'm really not cut out for this job? What if I bomb this presentation? What if I don't get the promotion? What if my business fails? What if someone knew what I really thought? What if others knew I was depressed? What if I can't make my marriage work? What if my children don't get into a preferred college? What if I can't lose weight? What if this problem really is my fault?

These kinds of questions, lurking about in our subconscious, cause us to hide, self-protect, and defend against our worst fear that maybe it's all true. But, again, we won't know until we're honest. In order to be truly honest, we need to separate the facts from the reasons, excuses, and stories we tell ourselves. Anytime something happens, such as my encounter with my boss, there are the facts of what happened. Then there is the narrative that arises in our mind, which is our subconscious way of making sense of what happened. It seeks to protect us from a negative outcome. In reality, we get stuck when we insist our narrative is the truth. We need to let go of the internal narrative that seeks to "protect" us. Then, if we look at only the facts, with no judgment, guilt, shame, or blame, we can begin to see past our blind spots and discover solutions that work.

I've worked with thousands of leaders over the years, journeying with them through the best and worst of their lives. Truth is, I've never seen anything exposed in someone's life that disqualified them from something better. Of course, there are natural consequences for our actions, and some of them can feel overwhelming. Still, our consequences will never define our lives if we let them become a doorway to a better version of ourselves.

> *Truth* is, I've never seen anything exposed in someone's life that disqualified them from something better.

AVOID THE GUTTERS

There are two gutters on either side of this pathway of Honesty: Projection and Self-Condemnation. If we're not careful, they are easy to fall into. First, we can look at any particularly difficult situation in which we find ourselves and project blame. This is the blame game. This was my initial response to my failure with the client. I blamed them and their dysfunction. I had convinced myself that I was doing everything right. I was completely unaware of how my frustration and anger were undermining the client relationship. The fear that I was in over my head and a desire to protect my perceived reputation caused me to live in denial. And by the way, we all do this when we don't separate the facts from the stories in our head.

When I think back on this experience, I knew something wasn't right in the relationship. I found it easier to ignore the signs rather than confront what I might find. When I realized my boss wasn't going to tolerate my excuses, I jumped back onto the road of Honesty, but found it too painful. Instead, I jumped clear into the other gutter of self-condemnation, flooded with all-too-familiar voices.

"I'm an idiot!"

"I'm no good!"

"I'm not cut out for this work!"

"I'm a failure!"

"I might as well give up."

These weren't the answers either. Both projection and self-condemnation are equally dangerous because, in their own way, they block us from *breautiful* honesty. Honesty invites us to stare our situation square in the face, regardless of what it might mean for us, trusting that personal transformation is only found along the pathway of *breautiful* honesty.

Transformation is only found along the pathway of *breautiful* honesty.

EQ CHECK-IN

1. Before we look at the second skill, take a moment to reflect on which gutter you are more likely to jump into when confronted with painful truths. Do you tend to lean toward blaming others or toward self-condemnation?

2. Who do you trust to help you see your blind spots?

3. When was the last time you asked someone to help you see your blind spots?

4. Do you have an accurate assessment of your strengths and weaknesses? Make a list of the strengths and weaknesses those closest to you would identify regarding your life and leadership.

5. When was the last time you were confronted with a painful truth about yourself? How did you respond?

6. Can you identify a time when confronting a painful truth about yourself led to personal transformation? What blind spot was revealed at that time? What transformation did this lead to?

KEY POINTS TO REMEMBER

- Honesty is the accurate assessment of your thoughts, attitudes, and behaviors along with how they impact your environment.

- In order to be truly honest, you need to separate the facts from the reasons, excuses, and stories you tell yourself.

- The truth will always set you free.

06

HUMILITY

The second skill of Self-Awareness is humility. But, before we dive into what humility is, let's take a look at what it's not. The oxford dictionary defines humility as; "A modest or low view of one's own importance." Although this, and other definitions like it, are technically correct, they leave a lot of room for misunderstanding. Too quickly, we associate humility with thinking lowly of ourselves. We find it difficult to embrace and celebrate the best parts of who we are for fear we're bragging and being arrogant. As a result, we tend to shrug off compliments by saying something such as, "It's no big deal" or "It was nothing."

Likewise, when hearing criticism, we struggle with seeing it for what it really is. A misconception of humility causes us to hear any negative feedback as a confirmation of our worst fears—that we are unimportant or not valuable. Humility is *not* thinking of yourself as lower than, less important than, or less valuable than anyone else.

So, what is humility?

If honesty is about seeing ourselves for who we are, humility is about accepting what we see. humility invites us to embrace the good, the bad, and the ugly of what we find inside ourselves. Humility is the ability to accept yourself as you are instead of who you or others wish you were. It frees you from an overly high concern with what other people think of you. Another definition of humility is "quiet strength." A humble person knows who they are, knows they are valuable, and doesn't need to announce their worth to the world.

Through humility, we can embrace all past and present areas of our lives—for better and for worse. Therefore, humility is about making peace with what is, not with what you wish was. As a result, this kind of humility unlocks our ability to see and step into the gap between who we are and who we want to be.

GOLD AND DIRT

Back in elementary school, I traveled with my class to visit a camp in Southern California where we had an opportunity to pan for gold. I was going to be rich! We sat through the glorious story of the Gold Rush of the 1800s, after which we were each handed a metal plate. The teachers pointed to a large trough filled with murky water concealing the riches beneath. We dipped our plates into the water, dug up some dirt, and began the frenzied search for anything shiny! As you well know, the tiny gold flakes we discovered and returned home with were of little value, but the experience was seared into my mind. In my later studies, I learned the extraction of precious metals, diamonds, and other gems often requires digging through lots of dirt.

Humility requires embracing both the "gold" and the "dirt" of our own lives. We are all works in progress. None of us is fully mature. None of us have fully arrived at perfection in any area of our lives. To celebrate the gold and ignore the dirt leaves us with little appreciation of all we've had to overcome to get where we are. We were born into the world with tremendous value, though much of it lay hidden and must be discovered. Our personalities, gifts, and natural strengths are examples of the gold we came into the world with. Our parents, family, friends, teachers, and coaches invested more value into us. Finally, every bit of learning squeezed from life experiences adds to our value. Every one of us is a goldmine!

But, it's hard to see and celebrate the gold when all you're paying attention to is the dirt. We all need to realize there is nothing actually wrong with us, even though we're not perfect. There's nothing wrong with the dirt and rocks in a gold mine. Those are simply natural substances blocking the gold. People are like this, too. Our "dirt" is blocking our gold, but that doesn't mean we're fatally flawed.

Honesty forces us to reckon with the dirt. Humility invites us to see every bit of dirt in our lives as an opportunity to discover more gold. True humility enables us to realize that our beauty is seen through both the gold and the dirt. Both tell the fascinating story of our lives, who we are, what we've been through, what we've overcome, where we've travailed. Every person's story, for better or worse, reveals incredible value amidst the rubble.

When we can accept the best and worst of our character, we experience the understanding that we are not all bad while

Honesty forces us to reckon with the dirt. *Humility* invites us to see every bit of dirt in our lives as an opportunity to discover more gold.

still being open to growth areas. The gold we see gives us the courage and hope to engage growth opportunities and move forward. Meanwhile, the dirt we see provides the perspective that we have not yet fully arrived.

If honesty confronts what we often avoid, humility urges us to embrace the possibility of greater things being discovered.

My boss confronted me with a truth I did not like. My poor performance, my failure, had resulted in a potential professional catastrophe. Dirt, dirt, and more dirt! At the time, I thought I knew what was next. I would be fired and shamed before all my colleagues. Word would get out, and I would spend the rest of my career clawing my way out of this pit of despair.

I'm still not sure how, but in the midst of all of my own internal chaos, I remembered something about my mentor. He cared more about whether I learned from my failures than the actual failures themselves. I reminded myself that growth *requires* failure. Children learn to walk by failing forward. They stumble, fumble, and bumble their way into their ability to walk. Can you imagine if every time a child fell, their parent reprimanded them? Or worse, can you imagine a toddler scolding himself for falling down? We'd all be crawling our way through life!

Thankfully, my mentor refused to let me get lost in the dirt. Instead, he helped me see that I was more valuable than my biggest failures could ever negate. I was more valuable than my biggest successes could ever add up to. He helped me escape being defined by what I had done and helped me to be defined instead by who I was becoming as a person. We would have to dig through the dirt to find more gold.

As with honesty, humility is bordered by two gutters. In one gutter, we turn a blind eye to our inadequacies and pretend we have arrived and have it all together. This leads to arrogance and robs us of any opportunity for personal transformation and growth. Arrogance breaks trust with others because it is a form of pretending. Arrogance reeks of inauthenticity and creates a culture in which everyone else has to be perfect. In the other gutter, we only see the dirt, which leads to self-abasement. We belittle ourselves and believe we are less deserving than those around us, causing us to shrink back from opportunities to contribute what we have to any situation. Both gutters are paved in distortion and judgement, neither of which are empowering or useful in leadership.

LET THE CHIPS FALL WHERE THEY MAY

When we're afraid we don't have what it takes or feel insecurities rising within us, it's easy to hold our cards close to our chest. *What if what I bring to the table isn't any good? What if my ideas get shot down? What if others realize I'm an imposter?* Practicing humility is simply playing your cards and letting the chips fall where they may.

Many of us struggle with an "imposter syndrome,"[9] a limiting belief that we've succeeded because of luck rather than the weight of our qualifications and accomplishments. I have to battle an imposter syndrome every time I prepare for a meeting with a significant client. *What if I don't have what it takes? What if I make*

_____

9 Pauline Rose Clance and Suzanne A. Imes, 1978

a mistake? What if I don't have what they need? The imposter syndrome, often rooted in "what ifs," questions our credentials and causes us to hold onto our cards for fear we have a losing hand.

Some years ago, I discovered I suffered from imposter syndrome as a parent. I was in awe of how my wife so graciously and patiently led our then small children. She seemed unflappable, even in the most trying times. On the other hand, I often lost my temper, barked orders from across the house, and complained about every toy not in its proper place. Compared to my wife, I often felt like a failure as a parent. *I'm not as patient as my wife. I lose my temper more than my wife. I don't know how to connect with my kids as well as my wife. I can't watch this Baby Einstein video for the 100th time!* The imposter syndrome can stem from unhealthily comparing ourselves to others, thereby causing us to shrink back from responsibility and opportunity.

But what's the worst thing that can happen?

We find an inadequacy in ourselves? We realize there are skills we need to improve on? Shortcomings in our character or our abilities are exposed? I don't believe these are our worst fears. I think, deep down, we all understand that personal growth only occurs in the areas where we discover gaps in our performance. I believe our real fears are associated with being demoted, disqualified, or dismissed.

Here's a thought: what if we embraced the idea that all we have at any time in our lives is *what we have*, not what we wish we had. Honesty plays the cards we have, and humility lets the chips fall where they may. Sometimes we'll have winning hands; other times we'll have losing hands. That's the reality of life.

Every winning hand is an opportunity to celebrate our growth, while every losing hand is an opportunity to learn!

The only way we'll seize the incredible growth opportunities in our lives is to surrender our fear of not having or being enough. We must play the cards we actually have, remembering that the only real losers at the table are those who refuse to play their cards and embrace every failure as another growth opportunity. The goal of humility is to embrace our best and worst qualities. In doing so, we find the freedom to be truly ourselves and an opportunity to become more.

EQ CHECK-IN

1. How comfortable are you acknowledging the gold in your life and leadership? Take some time to list your golden qualities and abilities. Don't be afraid to ask someone for help.

2. Do you tend to pay more attention to the gold or to the dirt in yourself?

3. Do you tend to pay more attention to the gold or dirt in others?

4. Describe a time when you discovered dirt in your life that led to an opportunity for growth. How did that opportunity change your life and/or your leadership?

5. Identify one area of your life where you struggle playing your cards and letting the chips fall where they may? What are you most afraid will happen if you brought your full self to the situation? What would it look like to bring your whole self to that space?

KEY POINTS TO REMEMBER

- Humility is the ability to accept yourself as you are instead of who you or others wish you were. It frees you from an overly high concern with what other people think of you.

- Honesty forces you to reckon with your dirt; humility invites you to see every bit of dirt in your life as an opportunity to discover more gold.

- The goal of humility is to embrace your best and worst qualities: no inauthenticity, no shame, no false pride.

07

SELF-LOVE

In 1955, Bobby Richardson was the rookie second baseman for the New York Yankees on a roster comprised of five Hall of Fame players. One of those players was none other than the great Mickey Mantle. Bobby tells the story of a very early game in that season that he credits as a breakthrough moment in his career. Bobby had just walked back to the dugout after yet another unsuccessful attempt at-bat. He was angry, throwing his equipment around, and mentally beating himself up. After he sat on the bench, Mickey Mantle approached him and said, "Rookie, you need to realize the best hitters in the game fail seven out of ten times at the plate. If you don't learn to accept that failure is part of the game, you will never last up here!" That conversation freed Bobby to accept the failure *with* the success, which enabled him to have a long and storied career that included three world series championships and a world series MVP.

Bobby's breakthroughs came as he stared the facts in the face, embraced the tension between his failures and successes, and persevered in believing he could do better. This belief in himself, which carried Bobby into even greater successes, is the practice of self-love.

BRIDGING THE GAP

At first glance, this third skill may sound a bit narcissistic, self-indulgent, or like pop psychology psycho-babble. However, there is a simple truth at work in this skill; you can only give to others what you cultivate in yourself. If we truly desire to have the skill to lead others to a better future, we first have to be willing to cultivate a better future for ourselves. Self-love is giving ourselves permission to release our past and press into the future. By practicing self-love, you will begin to believe in yourself and the better you of the future.

As I reflected on my failure with our ex-client, I found myself wallowing in the quagmire of shame. The feeling of shame came over me when I saw nothing but my dirt. Shame is that bottom-of-the-pit feeling you get when you believe your failures define who you are as a person. In this particular situation, I went from thinking I had arrived and the need for growth was a thing of the past to realizing my coaching ability had hit a roadblock. I went from feeling in total control of my situation to feeling there was nothing I could do to redeem my error. I had landed at the belief that my failure to perform meant I was a failure. Shame loves to convince us that our value is inherently tied to our successes and failures. This simply isn't true.

We have all felt shame when overwhelmed by the dirt of our life. Shame debilitates us when we allow it to tell us we are unworthy, of little value, or without hope because of our circumstances.

Shame can lead us to feel as though our whole self is flawed, bad, or subject to exclusion. It motivates us to hide or to do something to save face. Shame undermines self-love by making the gap in front of us look too large to cross. The power of self-love is that it provides a bridge that spans even the largest of these gaps.

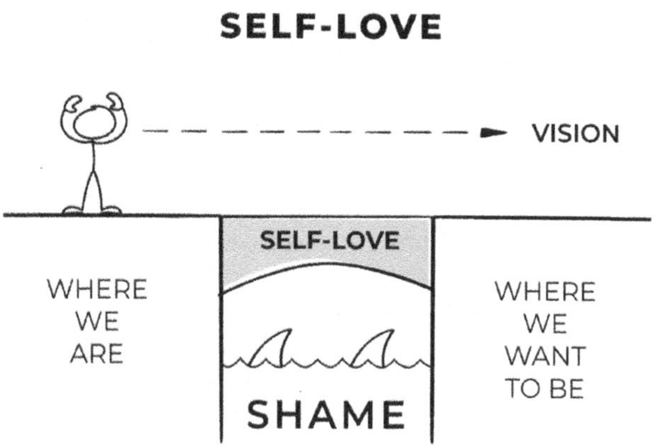

SELF-LOVE

Figure 11

Shame tells me I'm a bad person when I lose my temper with my kids. Self-love reminds me I'm not perfect, and I can become more skilled at engaging my kids with composure and flexibility. Shame tells me I'm worthless when I botch a presentation. Self-love reminds me there is much to learn from the disappointment and to keep trying. Shame tells me no one wants to read my book when I'm struggling through the editing process. Self-love reminds me that my voice is unique, and my own journey will benefit others. Shame tells me I'll never lose weight when I fall off the wagon. Self-love reminds me that if I don't give up, I can achieve personal change.

SHIFTING FROM SHAME TO SELF-LOVE

If left unchecked, shame will bury you in a pit of hopelessness and despair. It can fog your brain and leave you feeling powerless to repair your failures. Shame can sneak up on you so fast that before you know it, your survival instincts have kicked into high gear, and you're searching for a way to escape the humiliation you feel. One escape route may look like packing a bag and leaving town—not recommended. Another may look like attacking whoever triggered your shame—also not recommended. Your best escape is to shift into self-love. Only then will you have the clarity to address your situation enough to create a positive outcome.

So, how can you shift from shame to self-love and regain your composure? How can you stop pinballing long enough to think clearly about it? For starters, here are three steps you can take:

Step one: Recognize where shame has crept into your self-assessment. Notice the emotional and bodily sensations you're having. Take note of any shame-based self-talk running through your mind. (Hint: It will be self-condemning).

Step two: Recognize that you are reacting to something in your past, whether it happened three hours ago or thirty years ago. Remember, you cannot change the past; you can only make changes that improve your future. Choose to accept the *breautiful* honesty of both the gold and dirt, refusing to compromise one for the other.

Step three: Forgive yourself, face your fears, and forge ahead.

FORGIVING AND FORGING

For weeks I met with my mentor in an attempt to forge ahead and squeeze all the personal transformation that was available by practicing lots of uncomfortable honesty, humility, and self-love. I wanted to quit many times. Over and over, I ran into internal roadblocks. And over and over, he communicated that he was more interested in the leader I was becoming than the mistakes I had made. Finally, after several weeks he looked right into my eyes and asked, "What are you so afraid of?" I simply stared back at him in silence. For the first time in weeks, I had no words! The question hit me right in the chest. I was stunned. He encouraged me to dig deep and wrestle with this question and sent me on my way.

At the time, my family and I were living in an Atlantic beach town. I knew I had to get home that night for a work event we were hosting at my house. Leaders we had been working with all week would enjoy a final meal together while we celebrated what they had been learning. Talk about bad timing! I needed space to breathe and think about the question my mentor dropped on my lap like a bomb. I went for a quick walk on the beach. It was toward the end of the day, and most of the sunbathers had deserted the beach due to overcast skies. I passed by a few determined walkers out for some exercise.

What was I so afraid of?

I walked along, repeating the question over and over again out loud. I was hoping a voice from above would break through the clouds and enlighten me. The question bore down on me with incredible pressure. No answers surfaced. Finally, in desperation, I looked out over the ocean and began yelling like a lunatic at the top of my lungs. "What am I so afraid of? What am I so afraid of?" I am sure the few straggling beachgoers thought I had lost it. I didn't care! I just kept yelling over and over, "I don't know what to do. I don't know what to do!" I had no idea how to identify or escape the fear that had such a grip on me. But I knew deep down, this was a battle that needed to be settled if I was to move forward in my leadership.

Finally, I stopped yelling long enough to hear my own thoughts. Staring out over the endless sea, I began to hear, "Come in and die with me!" No, I was not suicidal. The words of Eleanor Roosevelt flashed through my mind, "You gain strength, courage, and confidence by every experience in which you really stop to look fear in the face. You are able to say to yourself, 'I lived through this horror. I can take the next thing that comes along.'"[10] Suddenly I realized the call to die wasn't about giving up on myself but an opportunity to *love* myself. What needed to die was the stranglehold my fear of failure had on me. That was it! I feared failure, and it had to die!

There was only one problem, I was fully clothed. I didn't care. I took off my shoes and started walking into the rising tide. But what about the dinner I was supposed to host? It could wait! A better, freer version of myself was in arm's reach. I was willing to do anything to get there. With every step into the water, I

---

10 Roosevelt, Eleanor. *You Learn by Living: Eleven Keys for a More Fulfilling Life.* (Harper Perennial Modern Classics, 2011)

felt the weight coming off. I continued walking until I was completely submerged. Call it a baptism or call it crazy. Either way, something was changing within me.

I was tired of being a slave to fear. I was exhausted with all of my own deflection and self-protection strategies. It was finally occurring to me how much energy I wasted worrying about what everyone else thought of me. Even more important, I was wasting energy hiding from myself. There is freedom in being who I am, for better and worse, knowing there is always a better version of me available. My greatest discovery - I didn't need to hide from myself any longer. I was free to believe in *me*.

Returning to the sand, I knew at that moment I had accessed and exercised a deeply latent power to confront my greatest fears. I was victorious! Sure, there was no parting of skies or crowd to applaud my triumph. But I knew when I walked away from the beach that evening that facing my fears and believing in a better version of myself would always be my choice, not a matter of fate. Failure would not have the final word in my life moving forward, but self-love would.

When we understand that loving ourselves is a choice we make, we are able to love beyond the shame of our past and into a more clear, confident, and courageous future. At its core, self-love is about the courage to forgive oneself. Self-love is choosing to forgive the worst we discover within and engage in the process of growth. Shame grips us when we choose to hold onto and give power to the faults and failures of the past. We have to acknowledge that what happened in the past does not actually exist anymore. The only power those things have is the power and place we or others give them. We cannot change the failures in our past any more than we can change what we ate for dinner last night.

At its core, self-love is about the *courage to forgive oneself.*

As I have coached people from all walks of life, I have realized we are much better at forgiving others than we are at forgiving ourselves. We so desperately want to be free from our past, but we hold onto it so tightly. We hold onto our past as if it's still happening. It isn't! The past only exists in our memories and our interpretations. The future only exists in our imagination.

If you failed at something, all there is to do is clean up the mess you made. Take responsibility for the impact you had on others. Then *let it go*. Forgiving yourself is the choice to let the past go, to be gracious to yourself, so you can forge a better future. That is self-love, and it will set you free to be the leader you want to be.

Forgiving yourself is the choice to let the past go, to be gracious to yourself, so you can forge a better future.

CULTIVATE A NEW YOU

Once you've shifted out of shame, you can simplify practicing self-love with another three-step process. First, you must *choose* to believe in yourself. Believe that you can become a better version of yourself. For this, you need a vision for your own growth. Identify the particular area in which you want personal transformation and make a decision to change. Remember, what got you here won't get you there, so you'll need new strategies to make the journey from where you are today to where you want to be tomorrow. Only radical change can help you get to where you want to be.

Second, regardless of the strategy you choose for transformation, you'll need to practice these new attitudes and behaviors. Very often, the prospect of change can feel overwhelming. You might think you don't have the time, energy, or resources you need. But long-term change is the product of choosing small behavioral changes and practicing them repeatedly until the new behaviors become automatic. It's important to understand that personal transformation more often comes from practicing new behaviors until your thinking aligns with your behaviors. In other words, you cannot think your way into new behaviors, but you can behave your way into new ways of thinking.

Third, after you've *chosen* to believe in yourself and you've defined the new behaviors you will practice, you must persevere. Continue practicing until these new behaviors become your new default way of thinking and operating. This is how the best parents train their children, the best leaders train their teams, and how you can train yourself into a new version of *you*!

> You cannot think your way into new behaviors, but you can behave your way into new ways of thinking.

GIVE YOURSELF PERMISSION

Every day I have the privilege of coaching leaders through the challenges of Self-Awareness. And every day, I relish the opportunity to help others practice the core skills of honesty, humility, and self-love. Whether I'm working with executives, entrepreneurs, managers, visionaries, or worker bees, they all share one thing in common. They're human. They get triggered, and they pinball. They desperately try to manage the controlled chaos until they get fatigued and burnout. They want more. They know there's more. The bravest of them learn to embrace Self-Awareness as a *breautiful* journey. They know it's hard, but it's worth it. They learn to give themselves permission to be on this journey and therefore create cultures that give others the same permission.

This is a journey, and celebrating the small steps is essential in fueling your confidence. Practicing Self-Awareness is no small feat, so encourage yourself and find others who value these skills and can encourage you along the way.

Pause for a moment and give yourself permission to be on this journey of personal responsibility. Give yourself permission to be a work in progress, to be learning and growing. Give yourself permission to be imperfect and committed to becoming a better version of yourself.

EQ CHECK-IN

1. What was your first reaction to the concept of self-love? Did it make you squirm a bit?

2. Is self-love a new concept for you? Have we defined it differently than you've heard before?

3. On a scale of 1-10, how confident are you about practicing self-love?

4. Think of a time when you failed at something. Notice what emotions arise with the memory. If shame is present, practice taking the steps to shift from shame to self-love. Give yourself permission to leave the past where it is and move forward.

KEY POINTS TO REMEMBER

- You can only give to others what you cultivate in yourself.

- When you understand that loving yourself is a choice you can make, you will be able to love beyond the shame of your past and into a more clear, confident, and courageous future.

- Give yourself permission to be a work in progress, to be learning and growing.

PART
03

QUADRANT 2:
SELF-LEADERSHIP

Practicing Self-Awareness to see and believe in yourself is the foundation as we continue the Pathway of Personal Responsibility into Self-Leadership. Self-Leadership is your ability to manage your internal world and operate in a way that is deeply considerate of the impact your presence and activity have on your environment. The real test of Self-Leadership is how you operate under increasing pressure when things are not necessarily going your way. Do you have the ability to maintain your composure when triggered? Are you able to flex appropriately amidst unexpected circumstances? You need to be equipped to engage the tensions that arise in any relational context to learn and grow through them.

SELF-LEADERSHIP

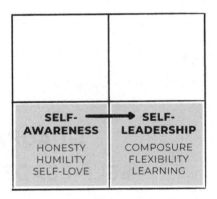

Figure 12

Ever wonder what happens when a leader is squeezed? When you squeeze an orange, you get orange juice. Squeeze a lime, and out comes lime juice. What comes out of us when things aren't going as expected, or life circumstances throw us a curve ball? Our true character comes out under pressure. By developing a more consistent character, our leadership gravitas increases, empowering us to operate with less fragility and greater poise under increasing pressure.

Self-Awareness is not enough. It is possible to get stuck in a kind of navel-gazing and self-preoccupation that robs us of moving forward well. We must pass through the territory of Self-Awareness into Self-Leadership to achieve personal transformation and develop a more robust personal character.

As you'll see in the chapters in this section, the foundation of Self-Leadership includes composure, flexibility, and learning. Self-Leadership is a prerequisite to effective leadership of others and a critical step toward taking responsibility for who we are and how we operate.

08

COMPOSURE

As I continued my learning journey in light of losing our greatest account, I came face to face with the truth of what happens to me under enough pressure. I lose my composure too easily. When my wife and I got married, I had a vision for how our household would be. Like many people, I wanted to create a more loving, gracious, and nurturing environment for my wife and kids than I experienced growing up.

However, the sessions following the client disaster exposed that when triggered, I was easily hijacked and would put everyone around me on edge. Furthermore, after an honest conversation with my wife, I realized I was also doing this at home. I had bought into the lie that I could compartmentalize my life, keeping work, marriage, children, friendships, and hobbies separate. I suddenly realized this simply is not possible. In every context, I found there was one common denominator—me. Who I am— my character, my habits, my gold, and my dirt—flows into every part of my life.

> Who I am—my character, my habits, my gold, and my dirt— flows into every part of my life.

Part of Self-Awareness is the courage to invite others to help you see what you cannot see about yourself. As I took time to listen to my wife, her observations hit me like an ice-cold shower. She graciously explained that when I feel threatened in any conversation, I become defensive, combative, and fail to listen well to others. She told me about her reluctance to engage with me on various conversations because my track record suggested I would get triggered, become hostile, and the conversation would spiral from there. She also shared with me that I lose my temper quickly with our children, who were four and six at the time. She observed that if a toy was left out, if the kids left toothpaste in the sink, or if they didn't respond immediately to my voice, I became triggered and barked at them. My lack of composure was creating the negative environment I was set on overcoming. My presence in the home was deeply felt by all, but not in the way I had hoped!

When we are triggered, composure is usually the first thing to go. The trigger comes in a flash, like a bolt of lightning. Before we know it, our emotions skyrocket and we find ourselves careening down the path of self-protection and negative default behaviors. We become disoriented and reach out for any means of regaining control over the situation. The need for composure challenges the control freak inside us all. Regardless of whether we fight, fly, or fold, these are all strategies to control our environment, to create personal safety, even at the cost of others. In order to recover our senses, regain emotional sobriety, and offer peace rather than anxiety, we must practice composure.

Composure is the ability to practice calmness of mind, emotion, and appearance under pressure. The best athletes, salespersons, executives, lawyers, surgeons, and parents practice the discipline of composure by communicating peace and calm in hectic situations. In other words, composure is keeping your peace when your circumstances communicate chaos. As leaders, we have the privilege of shaping the environment by our attitudes and behaviors, for better and worse.

My home became an incredible training ground where I was given ample opportunities to practice personal honesty, humility, and self-love. And, oh, how I needed self-love! My wife agreed to meet with me weekly with the expressed purpose of sharing with me where she saw me practicing greater composure and instances where I was not. She helped me process the factors that might be contributing to my lack of patience, such as over-working, poor sleep habits, and lack of exercise. Together we strategized ways for me to decompress more effectively so that I was better postured to engage my children with gentleness, kindness, and patience. Parenting became an incredibly useful context for me to practice greater composure and Self-Leadership. As I gained ground in that area, I became better at being composed at work.

> In other words, composure is *keeping your peace* when your circumstances communicate chaos.

SWAN EFFECT

To illustrate composure, let's take a look at what I call the Swan Effect. We've all seen images of the graceful swan in animated shows, while observing wildlife, or on nature channels on TV. They seem to glide effortlessly across the surface of the water.

They are a picture of tranquility and calm. What we don't see is all the work happening beneath the surface as they paddle to maintain or change direction amidst the underlying currents (see Figure 13).

THE SWAN EFFECT

Figure 13

As leaders, it is imperative that we develop our Swan Effect. We must learn to control our thoughts, emotions, and body language. During my journey of developing composure, it was a gift when my wife let me know I was behaving more like a dragon than a swan. When triggered at home, I was more likely to breathe out fire than gentleness. My wife and kids would kindly let me know I was losing my composure by saying, "Uh oh, Dragon Daddy is on the loose!" This was my cue to regain composure.

I'm not suggesting we stuff what's happening within and ignore what we're feeling. But we must resist becoming reactive, which often leads to unwanted behaviors and exchanges. Composure is the ability to remain calm and in control of ourselves.

In other words, composure is proactive. It is assuming responsibility for the impact our environment has on us and the impact we have on our environment in return.

Regaining composure often looks like giving myself permission to take a timeout. That's right, even adults need a timeout now and then! Strong emotions, biting comments, or raising my voice are the needle on my dashboard to let me know I'm triggered and need a moment to gather myself. I'll ask myself if my reactions are consistent with the situation I'm experiencing. I like to wait until my brain stops racing and I feel clear-minded before I reengage the situation. As a matter of fact, we encourage everyone in our home to take a timeout when needed. Timeouts are not permission to avoid conflict or withdraw from relationship. These moments are a strategy to regain our emotional and mental composure to bring the best version of ourselves to the table.

As leaders, it is always upon us to operate in a way that is in everyone's best interest. We do not have the luxury of losing our tempers, saying hurtful things, or treating others with anything less than dignity, respect, and honor. I know this is easier said than done, but *leaders define culture* for better and for worse.

How often have we heard these words tumble out of our mouth or someone else's mouth? "I only reacted so strongly because of what she said," or "I wouldn't have done that if he wasn't so careless," or "She made me lose my temper. She drove me to this!" Taking personal responsibility means we don't blame others for our behaviors, even when *they* are in the wrong. Leaders never play the victim.

Leaders never play the victim.

THERMOMETERS AND THERMOSTATS

Practically, there are a variety of techniques I have learned that help me maintain composure when triggered. First, know the signs that you are being triggered. We can learn to act as our own thermometer, knowing when our temperature is rising or when our thoughts are racing. Are you experiencing unexpected emotions? Pay attention to when your breathing patterns increase. Are you elevating your voice inappropriately, or is your body language becoming more aggressive? Are you no longer listening to what someone is saying because you're busy thinking about your rebuttal? These are all signs that you are triggered and possibly hijacked.

When you are hijacked, your amygdala—the fight, flight, or fold part of your brain—has taken over your ability to think with composure. When that happens, it's difficult to stop your own erratic reactions. You may say something you'll regret later. You may do something that damages rather than repairs a relationship. However, you can regain composure quickly if you can catch yourself at the first signs of being triggered.

Second, be your own thermostat. A thermometer tells us the temperature, but a thermostat gives us the power to change it. When you find yourself triggered, there's a good chance your next move will not be your best. Give yourself permission to pause, to collect yourself, and even let the other party know you have been triggered. You need an opportunity to regain clarity of thought and emotion.

Sometimes we're triggered for good reason. Someone has said or done something unhelpful, unfair, or harmful. In those instances, being triggered is just an indication that something is off and needs our attention. Either way, until we have poise and self-control, it is unlikely we will engage the situation constructively.

I have found great refuge in phrases such as, "I feel pretty heated over this conversation, and I need a minute to settle down so I can reengage well." Or "I'm having a difficult time thinking straight right now. Can we slow this down a bit so my brain can catch up?" To some, this may sound like weakness, especially for those who see every conflict as a battle that must be won, or for those who are afraid to be seen as soft, overwhelmed, or out of control. Choosing to pause a conversation is vulnerable because it's an admittance that we're triggered. It takes honesty and humility, but I assure you, my requests for taking a break have been met with understanding and patience by others more often than not. Even if others try to force the conversation or situation, I have found pushing the pause button for myself is always better than driving through rush hour traffic with no brakes, if you know what I mean.

Here are some quick and simple ways you can practice composure during pressure-packed moments:

- Choose your responses carefully. Don't allow your emotions to dictate your responses. It's OK to express concern, but it's best to avoid jumping in the drama ditch.

- Shake it off. Nine times out of ten, the problem isn't about you. If you take things personally, you'll find yourself triggered, hijacked, and pinballing.

- Check your attitude. Recognize when you're triggered and let it go. Notice your self-talk and refocus your thoughts toward a positive outcome. Give yourself permission to push the pause button if necessary.

- Be objective. If you can separate the facts from your feelings in a tough situation, you're more likely to be creative rather than reactive.

- Respond with confidence. Trust there is a way through whatever conflict has arisen.

- Be responsible. Assume responsibility for breakdowns *and* solutions. Step into honesty, humility, and self-love.

- Draw on past victories. You have solved problems before, and you can do it again.

Pushing the pause button for myself is always better than driving through rush hour traffic with no brakes.

DISCIPLINE AND DISCRETION

Some have interpreted composure as the skill of stuffing all your *real* thoughts and emotions and becoming robot-like. I promise you that's not composure because, over time, those suppressed internal realities will begin to spill out in unexpected and undisciplined ways. For this reason, we absolutely need an outlet to share the deep internal struggles we experience. We simply need to practice discipline and discretion in who we share with, when we share, and where we divulge our internal struggles. This is the work of creating our own personal boundaries to ensure that we have a safe space to do the hard work of Self-Awareness and Self-Leadership. In doing so, we become better prepared to lead with composure.

Find a *trusted confidant*. I recommend identifying at least one other person you trust to open up with and be fully transparent. This person should have the maturity to allow you room to be messy, to be a work in progress, and to say things out loud with the freedom of changing your mind. They don't need to have the answers for you, but they should be someone who has your best interest in mind and can help you process the events of your life for the purpose of personal learning and growth. Also, make sure this person knows how to preserve confidentiality and won't share your private thoughts with others. For this reason, I often recommend you find a processing partner outside of your workplace. They might be your significant other, a close friend, or even a helpful counselor or coach.

It's important to pick the *right place* for these deeper conversations. At the water cooler, passing in the hall, or a side conversation during a meeting are not the best places for deeper processing, especially since others may hear you or interrupt unintentionally. I recommend finding a more private location where there is permission to speak openly and engage your emotions freely.

It's also important to choose the *right time*. I have team members who will try to grab me for a deeper conversation right before I need to step into another meeting. I'm unlikely to be available to give them my full attention when my mind is elsewhere. Therefore, set a time that works for you and your trusted confidant so you can make the most of the conversation.

An ability to gain composure in any situation takes practice, especially if you are easily triggered and hijacked. You can't fake composure, but you can certainly work on getting control over your attitude and body language. According to *Forbes* magazine, "When leading—especially during times of uncertainty and adversity, crisis and change—you must avoid showing any signs of leadership immaturity or lack of preparedness that will make your employees feel unsafe and insecure."[11] When you master composure, workplace drama and stress dissipate, and employees feel safe. This is an important step toward becoming a leader worth following.

---

11 https://www.forbes.com/sites/glennllopis/2014/01/20/7-ways-leaders-maintain-their-composure-in-difficult-times/?sh=734991362157

EQ CHECK-IN

1. Think of a time when you lost composure with a family member, team member, or even someone cutting in front of you in line. What happened? See if you can identify what triggered you. What thoughts entered your mind?

2. What does it look like when you lose composure? What emotions do you feel? How do you generally behave?

3. How do you feel when others lose their composure?

4. Can you identify real consequences from times you lost your composure? Have you lost friendships or clients or team members? Have you broken trust with others by losing your composure?

5. On a scale of 1-10, how skilled are you at identifying when you're about to lose your composure?

6. What does it take for you to be your own thermostat? What are some practical ways you can regulate your heart rate, breathing, emotions, and thoughts?

7. Identify one thing you can work on to increase your ability to maintain your composure more readily.

KEY POINTS TO REMEMBER

- Composure is your ability to practice calmness of mind, emotion, and appearance under pressure.

- Composure is proactive; it assumes responsibility for the impact our environment has on you and the impact you have on your environment in return.

- You can't fake composure, but you can certainly work on getting control over your attitude and body language.

09

FLEXIBILITY

Having grown up an athlete and playing sports throughout college, I learned the value of cultivating flexibility in my body. We stretched before and after workouts. Every coach stressed the importance of flexibility to mitigate unwanted injuries. Flexibility is the quality of bending easily without breaking. I've been intrigued by the careers of some older professional athletes who seem to defy age to maintain successful careers well past the average retirement of others. With a bit of research, we find many factors at play. Still, flexibility is consistently a key ingredient to sustainability and longevity for athletes under incredible pressure.

For example, consider the careers of NFL stars Jerry Rice and Tom Brady. Both have performed at high levels spanning two decades in a sport known for its brutal impact on the physical body and where the average career is about three and a half years. Both athletes have testified that regular stretching routines have meant that they bend when most would break. The impact of a tackle in the NFL can measure upwards of 1,600 pounds of pressure, which has been likened to experiencing a car accident without a seatbelt! Not to mention the awkward positions these athletes find themselves in under a pile of men weighing many hundreds of pounds. You can see how flexibility is critical to avoid being broken under so much pressure.

> ## *Flexibility* is the quality of bending easily without breaking.

Most of us will never face the prospect of being tackled like this (of which I'm personally thankful!). But it helps us understand the emotional pressure we experience in intense conversations or meetings. A comment can feel like a blow to the gut. Wrestling through important decisions can leave us feeling twisted and contorted beyond what feels natural. Without flexibility, we find ourselves reaching breaking points in which we sustain injuries and, as a result, are more likely to injure others with our reactive words and behaviors.

A BREAKING POINT

As I continued to learn Self-leadership through Self-Awareness, I realized a very common threat to my composure was my lack of flexibility. I once heard a wise older gentleman coin this mantra; "Blessed are the flexible, for they are not easily broken." Well, I discovered that inflexibility in my leadership was contributing to a lot of breakage in my world. A moment of clarity came from one of our coaches.

A big part of my role in my former organization was to train and multiply coaches to do what I was doing. My boss and I had quickly realized that if we wanted to expand our business, we needed to increase the number of coaches who could coach our clients in the tools we created. So, I created a coach's manual outlining the coaching process through a series of modules. One of the values we had as a company was a low-control/high-accountability culture. I soon discovered that, as the number of coaches expanded, the more controlling and less flexible I became. Not only was I seeking to train coaches to do what I do, but I was beginning to demand they do it exactly *how* I did it. This was stripping away all of their ownership, personality, and passion.

On one occasion, a coach had the courage to bring a new idea to me. They suggested we give each coach freedom to choose which module was most relevant for the client's current situation. This would be instead of requiring them to follow the order of the curriculum. My fear of adding some flexibility to our coaching process caused me to tighten control and reject the new idea. This same coach brought me other innovative ideas.

Sadly, I resisted those as well. Over time, my fear of giving up control earned me an unwanted reputation among our coaches for being narrow-minded and unwilling to entertain better ideas. My rigidity began costing our team as coaches began to leave our team in search of a more empowering culture.

I have realized that overly rigid and controlling leadership creates a culture that suppresses creativity, innovation, and growth. If we can create room for flexibility by holding the people we lead accountable to our values, rather than controlling their methods, we can release the collective potential of the people we lead.

Flexibility is a skill. The key to practicing and mastering it is clarifying the values we seek to uphold while realizing different methods can and should serve those values.

DIFFERING EXPECTATIONS

As in the NFL, collisions occur in life and leadership when our expectations differ from others, and we move in contrary directions. At first, these differing expectations produce conflict. The more resolute our expectations, the more forceful the collision. Some of us try to dominate our environment while others withdraw from the conflict. Over time our capacity to endure such conflict wains, and it becomes easier to avoid those with different opinions. We can find ourselves moving further away from one another until relationships become untenable. Lost clients, broken business partnerships, divorce, and squandered friendships are often the collateral damage of one or both party's inability to practice a healthy measure of flexibility. In my last story, it cost me one of my best team members.

It's important to note that expectations are not your enemy. They are simply a reflection of your hopes, dreams, values, and desires to accomplish or achieve something. Expectations are the necessary energy to engage the world, to shape it, transform it, or protect it. My purpose here is not to make judgments about our values or desires, but to help you understand how the *rigidity* of our expectations may cause unwanted or misunderstood collisions.

> *Expectations are not your enemy.* They are simply a reflection of your hopes, dreams, values, and desires to accomplish or achieve something.

The diagram in Figure 14 illustrates the tension between rigidity and flexibility in how we hold our expectations.

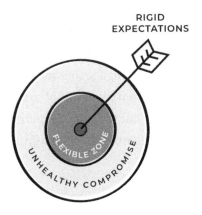

Figure 14

If you take the time to reflect on your expectations in any situation, you'll find your blue line, which is aimed directly at the bullseye of the target representing what you hope to achieve. When confronted by a differing expectation, you'll be challenged to move away from your initial expectation and explore the flexible zone. There is a measure of flexibility that will still allow you to hit your target, but probably not exactly the way you might want.

Flexibility will challenge any rigidity within you. When pushed too far, you'll enter the compromised zone in which you are no longer operating in line with your values and desires. The tension you then feel internally grows the further you move from the blue line where your expectations do not line up with the expectations of others. At this point, you are forced into one of a few choices:

A) Try to bend everyone else's blue line to align with yours

B) Consider alternative ways of achieving the same goal (Flexible Zone)

C) Find a different target that everyone can agree on

D) Find new people to work with

Flexibility requires a measure of compromise. I don't encourage the kind of compromise that feels like you're selling your soul. Healthy partnership is about identifying what *we* want to accomplish together and exploring a pathway that does not ask any party for unreasonable compromise. Whenever conflict arises in a meeting I'm attending, I like to identify the conflict and take a few minutes to remind everyone of our shared values and what we want to accomplish. Often, this brings clarity as to where the conflict is coming from, which gives us all the opportunity to practice healthy flexibility. It is important when collaborating with others to clarify the target, expectations, and values and seek win-win scenarios without compromising the organization, team, and goals. Emotionally intelligent leaders facilitate this space with composure, flexibility, and learning, which is our next skill.

EQ CHECK-IN

1. On a scale of 1-10, how good are you at practicing flexibility? Does flexibility come naturally to you, or have you had to develop this skill?

2. In conflict, are you more tempted to dominate your environment or withdraw? Why?

3. Where has over-flexibility caused you to compromise your values or expectations inappropriately?

4. Can you think of a time when you pushed someone else into unhealthy flexibility? How did that work out?

5. Take a moment to identify an area of conflict in your life caused by differing expectations. Have you clarified the target you are each aiming at? Have you clarified your expectations to each other? Can you find common ground in the Flexible Zone?

6. Learn to practice these simple questions, and you will discover the gift of flexibility. And remember, I'm not encouraging anyone toward unhealthy compromise. Too often, our fear of unhealthy compromise can cause us to entrench ourselves more deeply in rigid expectations.

KEY POINTS TO REMEMBER

- Overly rigid and controlling leadership creates a culture that suppresses creativity, innovation, and growth.

- Flexibility is a skill. The key to practicing and mastering it is to clarify the values you seek to uphold while realizing different methods can and should serve those values.

- Healthy partnership is about identifying what we want to accomplish together and exploring a pathway that does not ask any party for unreasonable compromise.

10

LEARNING

Learning, in my estimation, is a lost art. The traditional academic system in the U.S. is largely geared to help us increase our knowledge base gaining information, understanding, and skills for a particular subject. Knowledge represents the tools we need for building everything in our lives. We should do all we can to acquire knowledge, but it is not all we need for effective leadership. Having tools and knowing *how* and *when* to use them are very different things, as any master craftsman will tell you. We must expand our learning beyond knowledge and gain wisdom. Having wisdom is having perspective to apply knowledge in a way that creates the best outcome of any situation. Anyone can become knowledgeable about a subject by reading, researching, and memorizing facts. But wisdom takes knowledge and applies it with discernment based on experience, evaluation, and lessons learned. Wisdom always seeks the best interest of all parties involved.

One evening, I watched as my then three-year-old daughter reached up to touch the stove top, even after the many warnings

I had given her about touching hot things. She had acquired the knowledge common to toddlers; she had learned to use her body to explore her environment. But she had yet to learn the wisdom of when and where to apply this knowledge. This time I would let her learn a valuable lesson and increase her wisdom, so I said nothing.

Wisdom always seeks the best interest of all parties involved.

My wife looked up just in time to see our daughter on her tippy-toes, reaching upward toward the burners. I'll never forget her utter astonishment when she saw me sitting close by and simply watching the drama unfold. She screamed, "Eric, grab her before she gets burned!" I calmly replied in a way that reveals some funny differences between moms and dads, "But she'll learn a valuable lesson. She'll never do that again." My wife and I still disagree on this parenting tactic, but the truth is, she touched the stove, burned her finger, and never did it again. That evening, my daughter earned the gift of wisdom.

If wisdom is squeezed from the lessons learned from our life experiences, then the good news is there is no lack of learning opportunities. All of life becomes our classroom. Wisdom awaits us on the other side of our willingness to seize these opportunities. We can all point to these valuable life lessons that forever shape how we operate. But do we know how to "intentionalize" this process and squeeze more wisdom from our daily lives?

Let's look at how we can leverage what we've already learned about the everyday triggers we experience in order to gain more wisdom.

SPEED BUMPS

Every day of our lives, we meet with various triggers. Again, they come in all sizes with differing effects. Some triggers leave us with a smile on our face. Some are forgotten as quickly as they happened. Others leave us hijacked and pinballing. Triggers are like speed bumps. All of us have navigated roads with speed bumps. There's nothing worse than the one that surprises you by throwing your car into the air and testing the limits of your vehicle's suspension. We've all bottomed out at least once in our lives.

Life is a series of experiential speed bumps that can be rather jarring. But we have things to do, people to see, money to be made. Who has time to slow down? So, we speed through life, bottoming out over and over until we find ourselves broken down. And only then, when we're desperate, do we take time to learn from what happened. What if you didn't have to wait until your spouse files for divorce, your kids finally tell you how much they have resented your work, or your weight gain is threatening your health in order to realize that life isn't working for you? This is what happens when we have no practical handles with which to learn from daily life. We must become *learning leaders* who can pay attention to the speed bumps, slow down, learn, and recalibrate appropriately.

For example, one morning, I was late for a meeting and in a hurry to get to the office. As I sat in stop-and-go traffic, I found myself riding the gas and brake pedals, as if by my impatience, I could part the seas. My impatience was likely fueled by the terse conversation I had with my wife that morning about who was going to take our son to soccer practice later that evening. When I finally made it to work, I slinked through the conference room door and slid into a chair, hoping my tardiness would go unnoticed. Our team had assembled to problem-solve a communication breakdown between our headquarters and the hundreds of coaches around the country. Each team member shared their reflections and opinions about where the breakdown was occurring. In no time, the disagreements became heated, and arguments broke out.

The triggers I experienced on the way into the office were only compounded as I entered the fray of debate to argue my perspective. One particular colleague, with whom I did not often see eye-to-eye, took an opposing position. We argued back and forth until we were the only ones battling. My composure went out the window as I raised my voice, resorted to sarcasm, and began attacking my colleague rather than the issue. I had become inflexible and controlling. Not my best moment. Thankfully, someone intervened and suggested we pause the conversation and reengage the problem the following day, to which we all agreed. I retreated to my office in frustration. There I pounded out a bunch of emails and looked over some financial forecasts before finally heading home flustered and emotionally spent. And I still didn't know who was taking my son to soccer practice!

Let's be honest. We've all had days like this in which we bounce over speed bump after speed bump until we're physically, mentally, and emotionally exhausted. The problem I faced that day is that the next day would likely be similar unless something changed. And I knew that change had to start with me.

I needed wisdom. Later that night, I practiced the simple steps of a tool we call the Leadership Circle (Figure 15)[12]. I've used this system to train thousands of leaders to squeeze learning from any trigger experience in life.

LEADERSHIP CIRCLE

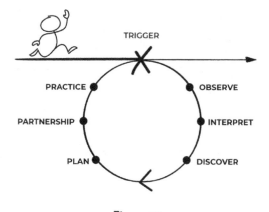

Figure 15

---

12 Adapted from Mike Breen, Building a Discipling Culture, 2011.

STEP #1 - Identify Your Triggers:
What most grabbed my attention today?

I took stock of any experience that stood out to me through the day. I asked myself, "What triggered me most today?" I remembered how I hit the snooze button four times, which forced me to rush through my morning preparation. I took note of the frustration and anxiety I felt while fighting traffic on the way to the office. I recalled being annoyed with coworkers chatting at the front desk and being frustrated with a superior for being unprepared during a meeting. I got slightly miffed during a sales call because the potential client backed out.

But the incident that stood out to me most that day was the argument I had with my coworker during our problem-solving meeting. This was the trigger that had perhaps the greatest impact on me that day.

STEP #2 - Observe:
What were the facts of the experience?

- I entered the meeting that day, already flustered from the morning commute.
- I had unresolved issues with the coworker.
- I had very strong opinions and bullied my way through the conversation.
- I lost my temper and became combative.

STEP #3 - Interpret:

Why did this experience affect me so much?

After some reflection, I realized that my need to win in every conversation left me insecure, and arguing more for my own preferences than for what was best for the project at hand. I was unnecessarily combative with my coworker. This was not easy for me to acknowledge or swallow, but I've learned that I am often my own worst enemy. I am naturally competitive, which drives me to succeed in good moments. In bad moments however, that drive causes me to fight blindly for my way rather than the best way forward.

This step often requires you to think deeply and be totally honest with yourself. Like I said earlier in chapter five, honesty is the first step on the pathway toward personal transformation. It can be painful, but it's worth the effort.

STEP #4 - Discover:

What insight can I gain from my interpretive reflections?

At that point in my life, I liked the idea of being a lone soldier, responsible for my own destiny, even when I was part of a team. At home, in the office, working on projects, and even while playing games with my family, it was difficult for me to see the win-win opportunities. I allowed my competitiveness to get the best of me while my behavior alienated and frustrated others. I am learning that personal success does not override team effectiveness. As the old African proverb constantly reminds us, "If you want to go fast, go alone. If you want to go far, go together."

The insights you'll gain from this step will arise from being honest and willing to admit your own ways that do not serve you or others. Once you recognize the role you've played in your experiences, you're ready for Step #5.

STEP #5 - Plan:
What will I do?

I should have told myself the following: I will apologize to my coworker for being overly combative during our meeting I will ask for forgiveness, and even ask for two ways I can be a better team player. I will say, "Thank you," regardless of my thoughts about his advice (this is still the most difficult part of learning for me—opening myself up to other's counsel). And I will focus on practicing a single behavior that will help me operate as a better team player. In this case, I committed to leading with better questions rather than assuming I knew the best way forward. This would encourage a collaborative culture in which we practice valuing each other's perspectives. More on this in the next section.

You will likely come up with several options for actions to take. The important thing to remember is to choose actions that both empower you and serve your team. Then you can consider Step #6.

STEP #6 - Partnership:
Who will help me?

Once each week, I could have asked a particular coworker how I'm doing as a team player and where I've been unhelpfully combative. Again, I will say, "Thank you," and continue the learning journey, sometimes retracing the six steps. I also need-ed to find a trusted partner to help me reflect on these areas of personal growth to keep track of how I'm doing.

STEP #7 - Practice:
Because practice makes much better!

I decided to continue practicing this new leadership behav-ior until it became a more natural part of how I operate. I've never grown in any area of life without a diligent commitment to practice what I'm learning. Real change comes from action as well as commitment. Most New Year's Resolutions fail because we fail to practice the plan and lack partnership to encourage us and hold us accountable to our goals.

> *Real change* comes from action as well as commitment.

Sometimes it's a failed conversation with my teenage daughter that most stands out to me, a biting comment from a friend, or a tired, passive-aggressive conversation with my spouse. Regardless of the circumstances, life is always happening, which means school is always in session for the Leadership Circle.

Excavating the learning is up to us. We're all busy prioritizing our days according to what we think is most important. Often, we unknowingly miss opportunities to learn what no book, conference, or report can teach us—how to lead ourselves and others better. But with practice, we can turn any trigger into a transformative opportunity with the help of the Leadership Circle. Figure 16 shows us how processing triggers all the way around the Leadership Circle changes our trajectory, leads to growth, increased wisdom, and a better version of ourselves.

LEADERSHIP CIRCLE

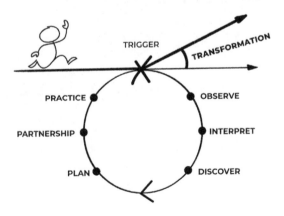

Figure 16

READY OR NOT (BACK TO THE MAIN STORY)

It was my inability to see others well that got me into trouble concerning my coaching failure with the executive team. I could not (and would not) see them except through my judgmental and prejudiced view. Why should I have to change the way I saw things? If I was coaching them, shouldn't they be the ones adopting the way I see things? Oh, I was so arrogant! Well, we know how that one ended. Thankfully, that failure became a doorway through which I learned to practice a deeper level of Self-Awareness and Self-Leadership. But, like any important lesson, you don't know what you've learned until it's put to the test.

After three months of processing and excavating the learning from my previous failure, I received news that a new client had come on board. And guess what? They were equal in every way to the importance of our relationship with the squandered client relationship. What an opportunity! Here was our chance for an immediate influx of cash, and success in this relationship would certainly open the door for many others. We rang the bells, poured celebratory beverages, and relished a second chance.

I entered into the festivities, but my mind was preoccupied with questions. *Who would coach their executive team? Who could handle this behemoth client?*

Knowing that a decision had to be made, I mulled over this conundrum for a few days. As the director of coaching, I was responsible for making sure we paired the right coaches with the right clients. But I was stuck. There was no one on my roster I believed was ready for this challenge. I couldn't throw any of my coaches to the wolves, so to speak. That left only two people: m y boss/mentor or myself. But I couldn't possibly suggest to my boss that I should coach this new client. The little I had already learned about them promised a challenge equal to the client I fell apart with. Certainly, he would think me arrogant for attempting such a feat. I decided I would let my boss decide.

I sheepishly entered his office, intending to ask him who he wanted coaching the new client.

"We need a win on this one," I explained to him. "You might want to ensure victory by coaching them yourself."

He never took his eyes off the papers he was reading. "You know who should be coaching them. Time to see what you've learned," he responded. He understood that our growth in Self-Awareness and Self-Leadership was only revealed by the tests that come in leading others.

Ready or not, I accepted the challenge.

As you continue to learn from each situation, you'll discover that leadership isn't what you do. It's who you are. And that's real wisdom!

• EQ CHECK-IN •

1. Now it's your turn. What situation, circumstance, or trigger can you process through the Leadership Circle above? Start a journal to record what you learn.

2. Do you have any other tools that empower you to increase your wisdom on a daily basis? If so, how has your leadership changed or improved in using them?

3. What significant learning have you excavated from life in the past few weeks?

4. Reflecting on the previous skills: honesty, humility, self-love, composure, and flexibility, is your struggle to practice learning possibly connected to a struggle in one of these other skills?

KEY POINTS TO REMEMBER

- Anyone can become knowledgeable about a subject by reading, researching, and memorizing facts. But wisdom takes knowledge and applies it with discernment based on experience, evaluation, and lessons learned.

- The seven steps of the Leadership Circle are a powerful way to squeeze the learning from anything in life.

- Real change comes from action as well as continued practice.

QUADRANT 3:
OTHER-AWARENESS

By practicing Self-Awareness and Self-Leadership, we have contended with what's happening beneath the surface—our own attitudes, thoughts, emotions and behaviors. We are now more available to engage the world around us with greater sobriety, clarity and effectiveness.

OTHER AWARENESS

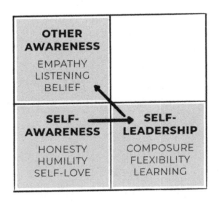

Figure 17

Remember, you can only give to others what you have cultivated within yourself. Now you can be proactive in how you see, interpret, and respond to your circumstances. Proactivity affords you a level of intentionality that can take you beyond accidental leadership toward emotionally intelligent leadership.

This next quadrant will equip us to leverage everything we've practiced in leading ourselves for the sake of those we lead. Through Other-Awareness we'll practice empathy, listening, and belief in order to develop the core skills to see others clearly and lead them effectively.

11

EMPATHY

Empathy is our ability to see and appreciate life from someone else's perspective. It does not mean we have to agree with them. But it does mean we make an intentional effort to understand or feel what another person is experiencing from within *their* frame of reference. True confession: this has been a tough one for me to grow in. Not only did I grow up with little understanding of empathy, I'm not naturally empathetic. That's two strikes! Looking back on my life journey, it is surprising to me that I was able to get as far as I did with such an empathy deficiency. Good thing empathy is a skill we can practice and learn.

SHIT FLOATS DOWNRIVER

At twenty-three years of age, I found myself emotionally, relationally, and spiritually bankrupt. My parents split up the year before, I had graduated college with no clue about where I was headed, and my aspiring soccer career vanished due to drug and alcohol abuse, which only exacerbated my already depressed state. During those pre-EQ days of my life, I tried to make sense of the pit I found myself in and placed all the blame squarely on my parent's shoulders. I felt my life at this point was the sum total of all they had taught me, so my own failures could only be their fault. Right? This worked fine until an early mentor challenged me with, "If you go on blaming your parents for everything wrong in your life, you'll never move forward. You'll stay stuck. Don't be a victim! Filter the bad and take the good. You're an adult, and you're responsible for your life now."

Growing up, I never realized my parents were aging. It was as if they always existed, and it was easy to forget they too were my age at one time. They weren't born into the world as adults! They had already lived multiple decades on earth. But it wasn't until my late twenties that I began to show an interest in what their lives may have been like before children. Whoa! The stories I heard about their upbringings—the good, the bad, and the dysfunctional blew my mind. I never knew. This was when I first realized shit floats downriver.

My parents were far from perfect, but they certainly weren't the worst. In hindsight, learning all they both had to overcome, I realized they did a pretty dang good job! My perspective of my parents changed radically the more I leaned into their story and the more I understood and appreciated what they had been through. Appreciating them didn't mean I had to adopt all of their perspectives, practices, or plans. But it did mean I saw them in a new light. I became less judgmental and more appreciative for how much shit they filtered and how hard they fought to pass something better downstream to my siblings and me.

We forget this is true of everyone we interact with in our daily lives. Every person has inherited generations of good and bad. It all floats downstream. The question is how much of the bad can we filter out and how much of the good can we pass down to the next generation? And who does this perfectly anyway? Exactly. Adopting this perspective by seeking to understand and appreciate others for the totality of who they are will serve us as we seek to practice empathy with others.

ASSUMPTIONS ARE A KILLER

Little else will quench empathy like assumptions will. Most of us are familiar with the saying, "You know what happens when you assume? You make an *ass* out of *you* and *me* (ass-u-me)." When we make assumptions about others, we find we're very often incorrect in whatever we project upon someone else. Making assumptions is like running through a forest at night with a blindfold on. Only danger and disaster await us.

In other words, *you can't serve what you can't see.* I spent the first few years of my marriage assuming my spouse pretty much thought the way I did. I expected (there's that word again) we would be able to make decisions together easily. I assumed we were coming from the same place on most issues; therefore, syncing and collaborating would be rather simple. Boy, was I wrong! It has been said that *our similarities bring us together, but our differences keep us together.* I knew opposites attract, but I was totally unaware of how different we were.

After three years of continual battle, we finally threw up the white flag and sought marriage coaching. There we were introduced to the fundamental skill of *empathy.* We learned how much we assumed we knew about each other's upbringing, personal values, and expectations. We discovered that we both assumed we shared the same goals and dreams. How wrong, wrong, wrong we were. As we practiced a learning posture, our empathy toward each other grew. Today we have a lot more appreciation, compassion, and understanding for one another.

In every client relationship, whether working with individuals, teams, or organizations, I see the toxic power of assumptions to undermine appreciation, communication, and cooperation. We come to the table with our own perspectives, paradigms, values, expectations, hopes, dreams, etc. All of these nuances shape how we engage problems, make decisions, and collaborate with others. However, the antidote for an assumptions-based culture instead assumes we don't fully understand one another or see each other clearly. This forces us to recognize that we're all different and we don't fully *know* each other.

You may be thinking:

"This is too much; it's overwhelming."

"How can I hope to fully understand anyone else?"

"It's too much information."

"It might delay important decisions or projects."

I'm not saying we have to know everything about the person across the table. But I am suggesting that a posture of empathy will go a long way toward helping us make room for one another.

Empathy builds trust because it communicates to others that we care about who they are and what they bring to the table. As I said in the last section, listening and learning about others does not mean we have to agree, but it does mean we work to make people feel heard and seen. You've heard it said, "No one cares how much you know unless they know how much you care." Empathy is the practice of caring about people, not just projects and profits. People who feel cared for will always be more productive.

How can you know if you're actually being empathetic? It shows up in the other person. When they get that you are working hard to understand them, they will let you know in words, body language, or facial expressions. You'll both feel a genuine connection. Believe me, acquiring empathy is a worthwhile investment.

Empathy is the practice of caring about people, not just projects and profits.

WHERE THE RUBBER MEETS THE ROAD

Back to my coaching story. It was not long before I figured out this new client was as challenging, if not more challenging, than the previous team. I found myself being triggered in the exact same ways. Frustration was a regularity as they came to the coaching sessions unprepared. Defensiveness crept up in me as they challenged the very concepts they hired me to coach them through. There was a constant temptation to give in to the triggers and become hijacked. The fear that I would buckle and allow my frustrations to take me down the exact same path I had taken with the previous client was unnerving. Would I succeed this time? Had I changed?

I knew I had a decision to make. I could walk down the same path. I knew it would result in another failed outcome. Or I could press in, take responsibility for my own leadership, and believe in the possibility of the client's growth as well as my own. For me, the choice was clear, even if it was a difficult one. To serve them more effectively, I would have to practice empathy.

I resisted the urge to make assumptions. I became more intrigued with why they would come to our calls unprepared. They were all very high achievers, so why did they push back so hard on concepts they agreed with enough to invest significant time and money to master? I began to see how this was unchartered territory for them. I could see their struggles, their fears, and their concerns as they slowly opened up and allowed me to see what was happening behind the scenes.

I led with my own vulnerability. When I could see one of

their team reluctant to press in further, I shared stories from my own journey. I shared my fears and insecurities. I shared stories of epic failures in my leadership. I shared both from my personal and professional life. My vulnerability gave them permission to be vulnerable as well.

I practiced being present with them in our sessions. This meant I had to slow my pace to serve their pace. I worked hard not to rush them through tools, instead focusing on serving them as people rather than a project. I listened intently, asked lots of curious questions, and gave them extra time when needed.

Creating a culture that was safe and trustworthy required I lean on all of my previously learned lessons. I had to trust that my previous failure would not define how this relationship would end up. I chose to love myself and believe in a new vision for my leadership, and I held onto the courage to see it unfold. I had to practice composure as I was still facing the same triggers as before. I had to be flexible as I faced a new pace that moved much slower than I preferred or expected. I had to learn a whole new way of interacting with clients. I quickly realized that this new client relationship was as much an opportunity for my transformation as it was for theirs.

I wish I could say it was smooth sailing from then on, but the next several months were sprinkled with challenges. There were many times I doubted whether success with this client was possible or even worth it. But with perseverance, the tide continued turning, more trust was built, and breakthroughs were beginning to be realized. As the weeks turned to months, we accomplished more than I could have ever imagined at the beginning.

EQ CHECK-IN

1. On a scale of 1-10, how comfortable are you with practicing empathy?

2. Does empathy come naturally to you, or did you learn this skill? If you learned it, how so?

3. Can you identify a time when your assumptions got you in trouble? What were the consequences of your assumptions?

4. When do you most struggle with being present with others? Why do you think that is?

5. Identify a time in the past month when you led from vulnerability. What was the impact upon others? If you can't recall a time when you led from vulnerability, think of a time you saw someone else lead that way. How effective were they?

6. Would others describe you as a curious or interested person?

7. How easy is it for you to imagine what life is like for someone else?

8. Try this: next time someone in your life seems upset, listen with empathy until you're certain the other person can confirm they feel understood. You may need to repeat or paraphrase their words back to them to show you're listening deeply. Notice how the other person's countenance changes when they feel understood.

KEY POINTS TO REMEMBER

- Empathy does not mean you have to agree with someone. But it does mean you make an intentional effort to understand or feel what another person is experiencing from within their frame of reference.

- Empathy builds trust because it communicates to others that you care about who they are and what they bring to the table.

- Resist the urge to make assumptions. Lead with vulnerability. Practice being present with others. Listen intently and ask curious questions.

12

LISTENING

There is a difference between hearing the words coming from someone's mouth and really listening to them. Unless you're hearing-impaired, hearing just happens whether you like it or not. It's why many wear headphones on a plane or in a coffee shop—to keep unwanted noise out of their ears. It's also why we may not choose to work while the TV is on or listen to the radio in the car while having a conversation. Hearing is an involuntary activity that we can only stop by covering our ears or turning off the electronics.

On the other hand, listening is a voluntary activity and a skill that can be learned and developed. Listening is the active engagement of giving our attention to another with the expectation of a response or action.

For me, it started when I was young. As one of four boys, my mother would literally have to physically grab me, hold my face in her hands and say, "Are you listening to what I'm telling you?" Of course, I was listening! She was shouting over all the noise my brothers and I were making wrestling in the living room.

She would then up the ante by asking, "What did I say?" I often stammered back, "Uh...Um...Uh. I don't know." That's the difference between hearing and listening. I could hear her voice, but I had no clue what she was saying. I didn't know how to respond because I wasn't listening.

Isn't this exactly what happens to us in particular conversations? We find the noise within our own minds or emotions too loud to really listen and understand what the other person is communicating. Maybe our boredom has given us permission to check out and think about something else. Or perhaps we're too busy thinking about what we want to say in response. We can easily miss whatever they are offering to help us understand and appreciate their point.

Listening is something we consciously choose to do; it's active. We choose to hone in on what someone else is saying and make every attempt to understand and appreciate what they are trying to communicate. If we adopt an empathetic posture, listening well becomes much easier. We're genuinely interested in what the other party is trying to say rather than our predetermined assumptions. True listening goes beyond hearing someone's words. It gives us access to understanding what's beneath their words.

WALK THE TALK

As a professional coach, it took me some time before I realized my job was to listen more than I spoke. In the beginning, I felt a constant pressure to say something clever or solve the client's problems. After all, they were paying me to coach them, to make them better. I figured more information poured into them would translate into learning and transformation. I was wrong.

As I spent months with the new coaching client, practicing empathy and slowly earning their trust, I discovered a new issue. Not only were they terrible at listening to one another, but I struggled with listening to them. If they said something I didn't agree with, or felt was off track, my instinct was to interrupt and try to guide the conversation back to where I thought it should be. Any trust I earned was just as quickly spent with every interruption. I began to notice the dejection in their faces when I interrupted. Essentially, I was treating them exactly the way I did not want them treating each other. Fail!

During this time, I happened to be reading Michael Marquardt's *Leading with Questions*[13], which further exposed the error of my ways. Michael does a great job of unpacking the power of asking good questions as a way of drawing out what's happening beneath the surface of any conversation. I wanted to control the conversations to fit my expectations, but I was learning how strategic questions allowed others an opportunity to discover deeper thoughts, emotions, and motives for themselves. I discovered it was much easier for someone to accept and own something when they discover it rather than having it imposed upon them by another. That was what they had been doing to each other and what I was in jeopardy of reinforcing by my own impatient leadership during our sessions.

---

13 Michael Marquardt, *Leading with Questions*, 2014

> It was much easier for someone to accept and own something *when they discover it* rather than having it imposed upon them by another.

But what if they don't figure it out? What if they never see what they need to see? What if they remain blind to what is holding them back or causing the difficulties? Well, as I practiced leading with questions, what I discovered blew my mind! As I suspended my own conclusions and learned the power of the WHY question, I began to see these leaders discover a deeper understanding and insight into the root causes of their frustrations. Asking questions helped them move together beyond the symptomatic issues to the systemic issues of many of their problems.

In one particular session, we were processing some of their team dynamics. One of the clients (we'll call him Chris) expressed exasperation that a recent meeting had been rescheduled. "I'm too busy to reschedule meetings constantly! The next time this happens, you can count on me not being available." The senior leader struck back with how busy everyone on the team was. Not being at one of their team meetings wasn't an option. Both parties were triggered, and Chris became increasingly hijacked. I watched as tempers rose and the conversation intensified. I could tell Chris was on the verge of saying something he might regret.

I felt my own emotions rising. But instead of trying to control the conversation as I might have in the past, I pressed in with a series of *why* questions. The intent was to give us a chance to discover where Chris's intensity was stemming from.

"Chris, *why* are you upset the meeting was changed to a different time?" I asked.

He responded, "Because now I have to move other important

meetings around to make it work. It doesn't seem fair. It's like a domino effect. Changing one meeting impacts other things on my calendar."

I pressed in with another *why* question, "*Why* are you upset that you might have to move other things around?"

"Because my week is already overloaded, and I can't squeeze in one more thing," he continued.

I pressed in further, "*Why* is your week so overloaded that you can't fit in anything else?"

Finally, he arrived at the root of his frustration. "Because I've been working overtime on a few projects, and they all need to get done this week!"

Now we were getting to the bottom of the issue! Chris felt overwhelmed because these deadlines had piled up on him, and he had no margin in his schedule to practice flexibility.

Almost magically, the rest of the team jumped in to affirm his work ethic and explain that none of them knew he was carrying this load on his own. The series of questions gave Chris an opportunity to mine out what was happening beneath the surface, practicing Self-Awareness and vulnerability. As the team members' eyes were opened to what he was going through, they responded with empathy. They listened as he detailed all he was shouldering that week. As a team, they began problem-solving how they could better support Chris and what items could be delegated to others. They all agreed to make sure Chris crossed the finish line that week with their help. Wow, what a turn-around!

After that coaching session, the senior leader pulled me aside to share his deep appreciation for how I handled what would have normally turned into another fight in their team. He recognized that his team was learning to suspend their assumptions and ask better questions to discover the deeper issue in any disagreement or decision-making process. He shared that developing EQ as a team was one of the most challenging journeys they'd been on, and he affirmed that it was more than worth it.

"Thank you for modeling the behaviors my team members are trying to learn," he said as he shook my hand.

"Believe me, I'm still very much on my own journey of increasing my EQ," I responded, then quipped, "I'm the proof in the pudding. If I can learn this, anyone can!"

LEADING WITH QUESTIONS

Good questions are one of the leader's greatest tools. Like an archeologist digging for valuable artifacts, pointed questions help unearth the deeper thoughts, questions, and feelings in another person's communication. No one articulates their thoughts or ideas perfectly all the time. As a professional leadership coach, most of my time is spent asking questions to help my clients discover solutions to their own problems. Good questions do two things. First, they help others mine out the deeper recesses of their thoughts and emotions. Second, they save the leader from having to come up with all the answers. An answers-driven culture creates codependency and shuts down creativity. A questions-driven culture creates an unlimited opportunity for the most creative solutions to rise to the surface.

> An answers-driven culture creates codependency and shuts down creativity. A questions-driven culture creates an unlimited opportunity for the most creative solutions to rise to the surface.

The best questions are open-ended questions as opposed to closed, yes or no questions. Open-ended questions encourage people to expand their thinking and explore what's important to them. They help to expose what lays beneath the surface of their own thoughts and emotions. I often ask, "Why do you think this is happening?" or "How do you think we got to this place?" or "What do you think is at stake in this situation?" My favorite question of all time is, "Where does the rubber meet the road for you on this issue?"

Others can tell when we're only asking questions we already have answers for. We call these "leading questions." Leading questions are the worst because they assume there's only one correct answer for any situation.[14]

Here are some great examples of open-ended questions from Michael J. Marquardt's *Leading with Questions: How Leaders Find the Right Solutions by Knowing What to Ask*.

- What do you think about…?

- Could you say more about…?

- What possibilities come to mind? What might happen if you…?

- What do you think you will lose if you give up [the point under discussion]?

- What have you tried before?

- What do you want to do next?

---

14 For a more detailed understanding of leading questions check out this informative blogpost: https://www.formpl.us/blog/leading-question

As you can tell from the previous story, *why* questions are my favorite because they invite the speaker to dig deeper for the core meaning of whatever they are saying. Asking *why* surfaces the deeper layers beneath someone's initial words. You can ask why to every response a person gives you until they've gone as deep as they can go. Those who know me identify this tactic in my leadership quickly and will often smile or giggle in recognition of what I'm doing. But they rarely complain because they have learned the power of the *why* question.

Sometimes asking why will unearth something deeper in the individual, and sometimes it will reveal something to the leader. In the above example, we discovered Chris' deeper anxiety rooted in his feelings of overwhelm when he had a strong reaction to a single meeting being rescheduled. Sometimes digging deeper with why questions can reveal an error in leadership. Imagine if Chris' final answer to the series of why questions had been, "Because he rescheduled the meeting last minute, and that's the fourth time he's done this in the past two weeks." If this were the case, it would likely be the senior leader of that team who would need to take personal responsibility for how constantly changing meetings adversely affects the team. Either way, asking why lets us to unearth the root of the problems we face rather than turning people into the problem.

True listening requires intention and commitment. When practicing listening, it's important to set your own ideas and opinions aside. Resist the temptation to take anything personally. Listening objectively can diffuse a disagreement faster than any intelligent statement. It can create more influence than any logical argument you might put forth. It takes practice to master the skill of listening to understand deeply, but the results are well worth the effort.

EQ CHECK-IN

1. Do you generally find it easy or difficult to listen to others?

2. Think of a situation in which poor listening got you in trouble. Can you see the difference between hearing someone's words and actually listening to what they said?

3. When was the last time someone interrupted you when you were speaking? How did that feel to you? Keep that in mind next time you're tempted to interrupt someone else.

4. Today, ask someone in your life if they feel heard, understood, and appreciated by you. Practice truly listening to them. What can you learn from their response?

5. Bonus points: Make a list of open-ended questions you can ask when trying to listen for what's underneath someone's words. (Hint: Borrow some from this chapter)

KEY POINTS TO REMEMBER

- Listening is the active engagement of giving your attention to another with the expectation of a response or action.

- True listening goes beyond hearing someone's words. It gives us access to understanding what's beneath their words.

- Lead with open-ended questions and set your own assumptions and opinions aside.

13

BELIEF

Believing in others is one of the greatest responsibilities of any leader. The very nature of leadership is giving others an opportunity to achieve something better for themselves and others. Children need their parents to partner with them toward maturity and adulthood. Athletes need their coaches to solicit greater performance from them. Team members hope their leader will help them achieve success. The responsibility of a leader is to believe in the people they lead and leverage everything they have to empower individuals to meet goals, achieve dreams, and go further than they would on their own. These are the kind of leaders I want to be around and the kind I aspire to be for others. The world desperately needs believing leaders.

But let's be honest, believing in others can be very challenging when we're seeing so much dirt! Whether I'm with my teenagers, my wife, my friends, clients, or my own team members, it's easy to focus on the dirt in their lives at the cost of the gold. Part of our human survival instinct is to always watch for what's wrong so we can protect ourselves. But that doesn't serve us as leaders.

The responsibility of a leader is to believe in the people they lead and leverage everything they have to empower individuals to meet goals, achieve dreams, and go further than they would on their own.

From our conversation on self-love, remember that leading ourselves means we bridge the gap between where we are today and where we want to be in the future. Believing in others is the discipline of practicing this kind of love outwardly toward the people we lead. If we cannot identify their gold (their skills and talents, potential, future, and better version of themselves) and learn to help them navigate the dirt, we are not believing leaders. Without this quality, we will find those we lead plateauing, frustrated, and eventually washed out.

Any skill requires discipline to develop. I had to learn the discipline of belief with the second executive team I coached after I bombed out with the first team. Though I was thankful for a second chance, I was deeply challenged by the difficulties I encountered with them. I was supposed to help them remedy their toxic culture (revealed in their very high turnover rate among employees and persistent dysfunction in how they communicated, solved problems, and made decisions). My job wasn't to teach them about the industry they had already climbed to the top of. I was there to help them develop EQ and increase their leadership gravitas for a healthier, more effective leadership culture. But, how do you believe in people who seem so far from the ideal? How would I model what it looks like to hold both their dirt and gold as I train them to bridge the gap?

SUPPORT & CHALLENGE

If you reflect back on the best leaders in your life (parents, teachers, coaches, bosses, mentors, trainers, etc.), the ones who empowered you the most are those who calibrated both high support and high challenge to help you achieve your goals. For example, imagine you hire a trainer at the gym. You arrive for your first session, and he kindly takes you to the smoothie bar. There he inquires about your fitness goals. He asks lots of questions because he wants to get to know you and understand what you're trying to accomplish. The trainer is kind, intentional, and attentive. He asks about your goals and struggles and empathizes with the failed diets and abandoned workout regiments you've made with every New Year's resolution. You likely feel supported by your new trainer. He seems to care about you, especially after he invites you to do a few reps on a few machines, but not enough to break a sweat. The session is over, and you think, *I can do this!* You go home feeling great about yourself. But what if every visit to the gym included the same experience? You might think your trainer is a nice person, but over time you're unlikely to make much progress unless your goal was to make a new friend. This trainer is all support and no challenge.

Now imagine the opposite experience. You arrive for your first session, and your trainer has already set goals for you, prepared an intense workout, and all this without having seen you or asked you one question. Every session feels like your training for a triathlon leaving every muscle in your body so sore you can't walk straight. You let your trainer know how much you're hurting, but he barks at you, "No pain, no gain! Pain is just weakness leaving your body!" It's not long before you feel discouraged, overwhelmed, and burned out. This trainer is all challenge and no support.

In both scenarios, your trainer believes in you and is eager to help you achieve your goals. But without a healthy calibration of *both* support and challenge, growth is unsustainable. Now think back to activities in your life in which you felt empowered. You grew, and you achieved your goals. It is likely either a leader or the environment provided the necessary support and challenge to help you stay the course, get the breakthroughs, and attain your goal. We all want the trainer who calibrates both well. They help you identify your goals, set realistic expectations, push you when you're tempted to give up, and never give up on you. That's a trainer who practices belief in you.

BELIEVING FOR BREAKTHROUGH

In one particular session with the second executive team, I could tell they were fatiguing from the coaching journey. The tools and skills they were learning tested their inner mettle. Every session felt like another trip to the gym to them. They were pushing their leadership muscles beyond what was comfortable or familiar. And in this particular session, I could see they were sore, tired, and burned out. In the past, I might have doubled down on the pressure and assumed my drill-sergeant mentality. But I had already reaped the consequences of this leadership style when the first executive team stopped working with me. I did not want to repeat this mistake by trying to break their spirit and force growth. I would need to provide a better calibration of support and challenge in light of the vision for growth we had all agreed upon.

As I recognized how challenged they felt, I chose to postpone what I had originally planned for this session so we could assess and diagnose their current status together. I led with questions to help them practice Self-Awareness and asked them each to share how they were feeling about the coaching process. They initially shared their feelings of fatigue and talked about how hard the journey had been for them. Some of them mentioned that they felt as if they were starting over as leaders, sharing how these new skills exposed inadequacies across every area of their lives. One participant even said, "I feel like I'm back in elementary school again!"

After giving them time to air their frustrations, battles, failures, and challenges, I asked them to remind me of the vision they had for their journey. They recounted where they were when the coaching process started. High turnover. Constant miscommunication. Relational dysfunction at every level of the organization. Distrust between team members. And an intensifying suspicion that their leadership culture could not sustain the rapid growth they had experienced in their industry. In concert, they shared that they wanted a healthier leadership culture. The team wanted to learn how to engage conflict constructively, problem-solve effectively, create a safe and trusting atmosphere, and build stronger team relationships.

As they reminded each other of their vision, I could see their faces begin to brighten with fresh hope. Almost instinctively, they began sharing stories of their own and other team members' growth along the journey. They pointed out in each other the breakthroughs that had already contributed to a better team experience. They encouraged one another, even celebrating how the new tools and skills led to greater clarity and a more collaborative approach to making important decisions.

They laughed as they recalled the more difficult moments when tempers flared and silly things were said. But then they quickly reflected on how they are all learning to respond to their own triggers with greater composure and flexibility for the sake of learning together.

I pitched in some of my own reflections, sharing where I saw important breakthroughs in each team member. I showed them how these breakthroughs were leading to the kind of culture I would want to be part of. By the end of our session, the vision for the journey had been restored. The challenges they experienced were supported by the evidence of significant growth. Everyone was reenergized and ready to get back into the gym!

Practicing Other-Awareness changes the way we see others in the same way Self-Awareness changes the way we see ourselves. Without a sober, accurate, and hopeful perspective, it is all too easy to give up on the leadership journey. But suppose we can develop our Other-Awareness muscles by practicing empathy for greater appreciation and compassion, listening deeply to avoid assumptions, and believing in a better version of others. In that case we will find ourselves postured to empower others beyond what they or we previously thought possible.

> *Without a sober, accurate, and hopeful perspective,* it is all too easy to give up on the leadership journey.

EQ CHECK-IN

1. Do you find it easy or difficult to believe in others?

2. Can you remember a leader in your life who believed in you well and helped you achieve a vision for growth? How did they calibrate support and challenge to help you achieve your goals?

3. As a leader, are you better at providing support or challenge?

4. How has a lack of support or challenge led to those you lead being stuck or plateauing?

5. Take some time to identify a vision for growth for each of your team members. How will you provide enough support and challenge to help each one grow toward their potential?

KEY POINTS TO REMEMBER

- Your responsibility as a leader is to believe in the people you lead. Leverage everything you have to empower individuals to meet goals, achieve dreams, and go further than they would on their own.

- Believing in others is the discipline of identifying another person's gold (their skills and talents, their potential, their future, and the better version of them) and learning to help them navigate the dirt.

- Practicing Other-Awareness will change how you see others in the same way Self-Awareness changes the way you see yourself.

QUADRANT 4:
OTHER-LEADERSHIP

This journey of emotional intelligence began with recognizing how often we are triggered, become hijacked, and find ourselves pinballing. Instead of blaming others and projecting responsibility on others, we have learned to traverse the Pathway of Personal Responsibility. Our path took us through the territory of Self-Awareness, Self-Leadership, and Other-Awareness. We are now ready to reengage the upper right quadrant of Other-Leadership. But now, we are transformed people, ready to engage our environment with increased leadership gravitas. We are less likely to be tossed about by every unexpected trigger. We can maintain our composure and bring a better version of our own leadership to every situation we encounter.

OTHER LEADERSHIP

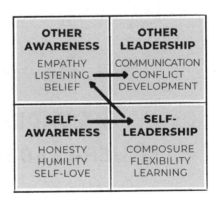

Figure 18

Remember, in our best moments, we intuitively practice all four quadrants. The pursuit of emotional intelligence is the process of *intentionalizing* this practice so we can engage more effectively and more often. This is the hard work of moving beyond accidental leadership to predictable leadership. A lack of predictability in how we operate creates distrust and instability in any context and culture we engage. The more we travel the Pathway of Personal Responsibility, the more we will be predictable. By practicing the core skills for each quadrant, we become trustworthy, and effective at leveraging the best version of ourselves for others.

As we enter into the final quadrant, we will look at the final three skills that characterize leaders worth following. These skills are incredibly difficult to practice if we have not passed through the other three EQ quadrants. But the more we have traveled the Pathway of Personal Responsibility, any fear, insecurity, or hesitation we may feel will certainly be alleviated when we enter the Other-Leadership quadrant. The three core skills of leading others well are communication, conflict, and development. Let's jump into them now.

14

COMMUNICATION

The challenge of communication is as old as humanity. I would dare say the best and worst human activities in all of history likely have communication as their one common ingredient. Nations go to war, marriages crash and burn, parents and children stop talking, neighbors feud, clients disappear unexpectedly, jobs are terminated with no warning, and on and on the story goes. These travesties are often rooted in poor communication. As I've said before, to accomplish any great thing in life requires we work together with other people. And that's where the problems begin because working with others means we have to communicate. As you know, this is easier said than done.

If you've had the privilege of traveling out of your own country (or even to a region with a different dialect), then you know how important communication is. I traveled through the Eastern part of India years ago on a humanitarian trip, and I remember thinking, *If I get lost, I'm done for!* I couldn't read any of the signs, and no one I met spoke English. For that reason, we only traveled with an interpreter who could bridge the communication gap. Without the interpreter, I'd likely still be wandering around the Nepalese mountains!

Another time, while speaking at a large conference, I attempted to impress some newly made British friends by bridging the communication gap. I decided to use language familiar to their native culture. I shared how important it was during any conflict to pause and reflect on the conversation with *tea and strumpets*. As you know, the British are fond of their tea. Afterward, my British friends were quick to point out that the proper phrase is *tea and crumpets*, not *tea and strumpets*. Strumpets are female prostitutes, not the wonderful little cakes I had come to love during my visits to England. That story is still told in many pubs across the UK today.

Nowhere has the battle for clear communication been more apparent than in my marriage. My wife and I had fallen madly in love, and I believed the electric connection we shared would be enough to see us through anything. Boy, was I wrong! The honeymoon phase quickly gave way to the "Oh crap! What did we do?" phase. Our arguments regularly devolved into *how* we were arguing about what we were arguing about! If you've been married longer than a minute, you know what I'm talking about. We knew how to communicate with each other when things were good (and as long as we generally agreed on the subject). But a little disagreement was all it took to send us into the throws of another verbal battle.

After lamenting to a friend about our failed attempts at communication, he turned me on to John Gray's book, *Men Are from Mars, Women Are from Venus,* which is all about communication. The book's main point teaches us we cannot assume others think, feel, or communicate the same way we do. Men and women share much in common. But we also share many differences in how we perceive, interpret, and engage the world—especially how we communicate. My wife and I can be looking at the same issue but communicate in a way that leaves us both feeling as if we're talking about two different things. The same can be said of any two human beings trying to get on the same page. Communication is hard!

Thankfully, Gray's book introduced us to new vocabulary, words, phrases, and illustrations that gave us a common language. With a little bit of practice, our communication began to change. We could finally understand and appreciate each other in a new way. We were finally speaking the same language! Having a shared language has become paramount to all the coaching I offer to leaders and teams.

SHARED LANGUAGE

Communication is a "process by which information is exchanged between individuals through a common system of symbols, signs or behaviors."[15] The operative phrase here is *common system*. The beautiful people of Eastern India, along with my wife, co-workers, and clients all have a system of communication. The breakdown happens where their systems differ from ours.

---

15 Merriam-Webster Dictionary https://www.merriam-webster.com/dictionary/Communication

What happens when we speak two different languages? Both may be equally effective systems, but they cannot communicate with each other. What happens when we use the same words but mean two entirely different things? Again, a breakdown in communication ensues. This is why we teach our children our family's shared language from a young age, and we ascribe meaning to this language to increase our ability to communicate, understand one another, and partner together in our daily activities.

As leaders, it is our responsibility to provide a shared language for the people we work with. We must decide on the language we will or will not use and ascribe meaning to those words so we can all get on the same page. Do we share the same vision, mission, and values? Does everyone know this language and what it means in a practical sense? Is there any accountability for the use of our shared language? Is everyone playing by the same rules of engagement?

One of our clients manages NBA teams. They said it best— "Our coaches would never put players out on the court without everyone knowing the playbook." The playbook is their shared language. If the best teams in the world with the best players in the world need a shared language to accomplish their goals, I can assure you the same goes for any other partnership.

A shared language or playbook creates shared rules of engagement. In a recent coaching cohort, one of our clients exclaimed, "I get it! I now know why there is so much conflict in my team. There are no shared rules of engagement. Everyone approaches problem-solving, decision-making, and conflict resolution with very different rules and expectations. It's like we're all speaking different languages!" For this reason, we work very hard to provide leadership communities with simple, visual tools to establish and reinforce the best practices for leading ourselves and others. We need a playbook!

I spend much of my time helping leaders and teams develop their playbook. I help them clarify their mission and develop behavioral values. We equip them with simple, practical tools that help everyone involved get on the same page when it comes to important activities such as: how they learn together, make decisions, resolve conflict, develop and deploy team members, communicate with clear expectations, represent the company culture, and so much more.

Very often, the leaders I work with already have some tools and shared language. Our job isn't to completely change what already exists but to make sure everyone is clear on what their shared language and practices are. Then we help them fill any gaps.

ACCOUNTABILITY

Years ago, one of my board members attempted to have me fired. At the time, it would have been easy for the other board members to feel as if they had to choose sides. Would they stand with their fellow board member or support me—their newly appointed CEO? This is often what happens in conflict; we choose sides. There's a winner and a loser. But that instance was different because one of the first things I did upon taking the helm was establish a shared language to handle any conflict.

One of our rules of engagement when conflict arises was to practice our three steps for healthy conflict resolution. First, if you have a conflict with someone, take it to them privately and make every attempt to resolve the matter with grace and generosity. If that didn't work, our second course of action is to invite a trusted third party to help us pursue clarity and reconciliation. If step two failed to resolve the issue, then the third step was to bring the issue to a person or team that both parties are submitted to for arbitration. That method of resolving conflict did not tolerate gossip, back-channel drama, or any type of processing without the purpose of promoting healthy communication, peace, and reconciliation.

Our board had committed to this three-step process as our shared language and practice for the entire organization. It had been introduced at every level of leadership, and the board itself was prepared to be accountable for operating in this way. So, when a particular board member brought his case against me, the other members asked him a simple question. "Have you done everything in your power to resolve your issues privately with Eric?"

He stammered, "No, because he wouldn't listen anyway. He's arrogant and young and thinks he knows everything!"

They persisted in explaining to him that if he felt threatened by me, he was welcome to invite a trusted third party to help seek a resolution. They also pointed out that he had skipped the first two steps of our conflict resolution process and needed to honor the rules of engagement we had all agreed upon. His unwillingness to operate by our playbook led to his inevitable departure from the board. A unified team is always better than a gifted team without unity.

A *unified team* is always better than a gifted team without unity.

In the same way I do with all my coaching clients, our board continued to establish shared language. That language has become our playbook for resolving conflict, making important decisions, and recruiting, training, deploying, and reviewing our leaders, teams, and our organization as a whole. I celebrate today that our board and leadership culture across the organization is healthy, vibrant, and has practical handles for healthy communication. We're all rowing in the same direction. We have shared expectations and rules of engagement because we're all accountable to the same playbook.

THE EQ MATRIX

Now imagine if everyone in your home or team had the EQ Matrix. What if everyone was growing in their ability to identify and engage triggers effectively? What if we all put the blame game aside and practiced personal responsibility? In our conversations, we could help each other pursue Self-Awareness and Self-Leadership. We would be able to help ourselves and others diagnose which skill we're struggling to exercise, then build these leadership muscles together.

Having a shared language means we spend less time speaking around each other and more time helping each other. I often pause to let my wife know I'm triggered in a conversation and need a few minutes to compose myself. I help her process when she's tempted to lose composure with her colleagues, friends, or our kids. We pull out the playbook and together assess where the deeper problem may lie, which quadrant we may be stuck in, and how we can take greater personal responsibility.

My teenagers know the EQ Matrix and often share stories of how they're helping their friends process conflicts with other peers and their parents. I often tease my daughter that she's well on her way to taking over my coaching business! Both of our kids practice an uncommon degree of emotional intelligence for their age. We've got a lot to learn as parents, but our commitment to introducing this shared language into our household means we enjoy working together far more than we work against each other. Shared language enhances communication which empowers partnership.

EQ CHECK-IN

1. When was the last time you encountered a serious communication gap? What were the consequences?

2. Does your team or organization have an intentional shared language? What are your team's (or family's) mission and behavioral values? Is everyone committed to the same playbook?

3. If you don't already have a playbook, take some time this week to create one for yourself, your marriage, your family, or your team.

4. If you're unsure where to start, contact my team at **mpwrcoaching.com** to discover one of the most effective leadership playbooks.

KEY POINTS TO REMEMBER

- As a leader, it is your responsibility to provide a shared language for the people you work with. You must decide on the language you will or will not use and ascribe meaning to those words so everyone can get on the same page.

- A unified team is always better than a gifted team without unity.

- Shared language enhances communication and empowers practical partnership.

15

CONFLICT

Conflict has become one of those *four letter words* that, for most people, immediately solicits a plethora of intense emotions. I have met few leaders who truly enjoy conflict. And if they did, it was likely because conflict allowed them to show off their battle skills, taking others down with their argumentative prowess or positional authority. As long as we see conflict as a threat to our or someone else's best interest, we will avoid it or seek to circumvent situations where it arises. But what if we saw conflict differently? What if we could learn to see conflict as a gift to ourselves and others, an opportunity for growth and creative solutions, instead of a threat?

Conflict is defined as a "collision or disagreement, when opinions are contradictory, at variance or in opposition; a clash; to fight or contend; to do battle."[16] No wonder we avoid conflict when it's defined as such violence! Sadly, this definition resonates with the terrible track record most of us have when expe-

---

16 https://www.dictionary.com/browse/conflict?s=t

riencing conflict. As such, it's difficult at first to see conflict as a beneficial skill to master.

My track record started when I was a child, listening to my parents scream at each other, doors slamming, objects thrown across rooms, and fist-sized holes left in walls. In my early years, my father "resolved" conflict by using physical and verbal intimidation to win his side. My mother chose a more passive and manipulative tactic. Neither was helpful. Unfortunately, their poor example was reinforced by bullies at school, passive-aggressive teachers, domineering coaches, and a long list of distinguished bosses. They all saw conflict as an evil to be smothered rather than an opportunity for something better to emerge.

I'd like you to consider that conflict is neither good nor bad, it is only an indicator of differing opinions. Conflict is just another speed bump, a trigger that lets us know there's always more than one way to see anything. Conflict is not the enemy, but how we handle conflict can be. I believe every conflict can be seen either as an *obstacle* or an *opportunity*. If seen as an obstacle, we might see it as a win-lose battle in which one party must overcome the other until they get their way. Or we might see it as a lose-lose situation where both parties decide a partnership is untenable concerning the issue at hand. What if we could see conflict as a *win-win* opportunity in which our conflict exposes possibilities currently unknown to both parties?

I am convinced our greatest adversary is not conflict, but the lack of skills we have to engage conflict well to squeeze the learning, growth, and collaboration out of any disagreement. If this is starting to sound a bit like what we've talked about throughout this entire book, you are correct. Every conflict is an opportunity to practice Self-Awareness, Self-Leadership, Other-Awareness, Other-Leadership and whatever shared language we have for communicating to learn, rather than getting our way.

Let's see how it all works together...

> Conflict is not the enemy, *but how we handle conflict can be.*

EMOTIONALLY INTELLIGENT CONFLICT ENGAGEMENT

The look on my team members' faces was priceless when, after a recent review of our playbook for emotionally intelligent conflict engagement, I gave them an assignment. "OK," I said, "your homework this week is to identify an unresolved conflict with someone else and initiate healthy conflict engagement. This is the first step in our agreed process for engaging healthy conflict resolution. Remember, engage to learn rather than to win."

I then reminded them that leveraging the Leadership Circle in their conversations to squeeze out the possible learning was their best tactic. I also reminded them practice makes better, and we would review our experiences the following week.

Later that day, I was pleasantly surprised to receive a message from one of the team members who said he would like to initiate conflict engagement with me. I was so proud of him for initiating this meeting as I spend quite a bit of time making sure our team embodies the values and practices we coach others on to increase their leadership gravitas.

This particular individual joined our team a year earlier and quickly discovered he was uncomfortable with conflict, particularly with authority figures. So, we set a meeting for the following morning. I'm sure he didn't sleep well, but setting a day and time to engage conflict encourages us to set our expectations aside. That way we can come to a conversation better prepared, rather than springing conflict on each other.

The next morning, he sat nervously in my office, waiting for our meeting to begin. I started our time together by drawing the Leadership Circle on the whiteboard and reminding us of the seven steps of learning we like to use in conflict-oriented conversations. This is part of our playbook. They are the same handles we use for learning in any context, which I illustrated earlier in the section on Learning.

THE LEADERSHIP CIRCLE

LEADERSHIP CIRCLE

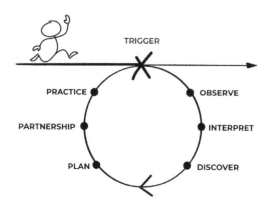

Figure 19

These words represent our shared language and create shared expectations for how we engage conflict together.

I started in, "So, what's up, buddy?"

After hemming and hawing for a bit, he finally came out with it. "I was triggered their other day when you barged into my office to talk with another team member about what photos you were going to hang on your office wall."

I sat for a moment, trying to recollect the crime. I encouraged him to continue as he had stated the conflict clearly. I asked him to *observe* for me what happened from his perspective.

He explained, "I only have my team together once a week, and we had lots of important details to discuss. We left the door open because it was warm in the room. In passing by my office, you looked in and caught the eye of another team member. You didn't knock on the door or ask if you could interrupt. You just interrupted and carried on for quite a few minutes in a conversation that had nothing to do with our agenda."

As he recounted what happened, I knew I had blown it, but I could also feel a bit of pride well up. I thought to myself, *I'm the leader. I can do what I want, right?* I quickly pushed this thought aside in favor of honesty, humility, and self-love. I thought to myself, *Eric, be ready to take 100% personal responsibility and stay in a learning posture!* I've learned the power of coaching myself, even during more intense situations. The EQ Matrix is burned into my mind, so I walked myself through the Pathway of Personal Responsibility. I wanted to ensure I was practicing what I preached.

I asked him how he felt about what happened. He shared, "I felt disrespected, frustrated, and hijacked for the rest of the meeting. It felt unfair."

"I really appreciate you bringing this to my attention," I responded. "I'm so sorry for how my actions made you feel. I love you and respect you, and want to honor you. I'd love to hear more about how you *interpreted* this experience."

"You have set the rules of engagement in our office," he continued. "You've asked all of us to show the utmost honor and respect for each other's meetings and to make sure we do not barge into meetings. So, either you're above the law, or you broke one of our shared office values."

We processed the event for a few more minutes which allowed me to practice empathy, listening, and belief. I knew he meant well, and this conversation was incredibly difficult for him. But our relationship was more important than protecting my ego. I confessed, "I'm so sorry. You're absolutely right! I did break one of our rules of engagement, and I blew it. I'm not above the law and want to honor you in the same way I ask you to honor the rest of our team." He smiled and shared how much he appreciated my response.

"What are we *discovering* here," I asked, "and what is your takeaway from this conflict?"

He responded, "First, I was so nervous about bringing this conflict to you because I was afraid you might just run roughshod over me. That's part of my past experience with leaders. Second, I'm learning that this tool really works! I get so flustered dealing with conflict and become disoriented. Eventually, I bail on the process altogether. The tool gave me practical handles and a clear road map to seek a win-win solution. I think we're both learning something here."

Then I asked, "So, what's next?" I was testing to see if he would stop at this point or push the conflict all the way through the process. Now that we learned something together, we needed a way forward together. We needed a *plan*.

He smiled at me again, knowing exactly what I was doing. "Let's make a plan for how we can move forward."

"Great!" I replied. We set a plan for how I would work hard to honor our agreed-upon rules of engagement in the office. We also set a plan for how he could gently remind me in the moment if or when I blew it again. He would be my *partner* in this *plan*, and we would *practice* it together.

In our culture, we choose to see conflict as stepping stones rather than stumbling blocks. We give each other grace to learn and space to be imperfect. As long as the person is genuinely committed to growing and increasing their own leadership gravitas, we stay committed to one another's journey.

CONFLICTING FOR A RESILIENT CULTURE

I like to think of conflict as a verb: *conflicting.* Transforming conflict into a verb moves it away from being a "thing" looming in the darkness, something to be feared. Instead, conflict engagement is an action, a process, a skill we can develop—not a tyrant to be avoided.

Conflicting with our Leadership Circle opens up win-win opportunities. I'm not asking either party in conflict to simply acquiesce their position or give in to unhealthy compromise, which leads to a win-lose. Instead, by conflicting with a genuine willingness to learn from the other party, we open ourselves to information or perspectives we didn't previously have. The smartest person in the room isn't the one with all the answers, but the one who is ready and willing to learn from everyone else. Conflict signals to us there is potentially more information, valuable perspectives, and helpful insights available in the room. By assuming a learning posture as a conflicting strategy, we communicate to others that we value their contribution and believe we are better together.

Conflicting well is the secret to a resilient culture. I work with people on teams who cannot achieve the necessary breakthroughs for successful partnerships. They are relationally fragile as everyone tiptoes around everyone else, fearing the next conflict will cause jarring conversations and further distrust. Fear of conflict will undermine our ability to collaborate effectively, which is the only pathway for successful partnership in any team environment. With shared language and rules of engagement, we can overcome our fears of conflict, build a resilient culture, and collaborate more effectively. It's not easy, but it's worth it!

> *The smartest person* in the room isn't the one with all the answers, but the one who is ready and willing to learn from everyone else.

EQ CHECK-IN

1. What is your history with conflict? Was it modeled well or poorly in your upbringing?

2. Do you avoid conflict? Why or why not?

3. What particular memories or relationships of poor conflict engagement cause you to fear conflicting?

4. Which of this chapter's tools and processes for engaging conflict resonate most with you?

5. Take time to reflect on a recent moment of conflict that did not go well. How did you and the other party involved behave during the conflict? What were the consequences? Can you imagine utilizing the six steps of learning to engage this same conflict? Take it a step further and attempt to reengage the conflict with the other party using this new process.

KEY POINTS TO REMEMBER

- When you learn to see conflict as a gift to yourself and others, you'll experience it as an opportunity for growth and creative solutions.

- Conflict is a signal that there is potentially more information, valuable perspectives, and helpful insights available in the room. By assuming a learning posture as a conflicting strategy, you communicate to others that you value their contribution and believe you are all better together.

- Conflicting well is the secret to a resilient culture.

16
DEVELOPMENT

Our final skill for practicing EQ is the pinnacle of all great leadership. I define great leadership as the ability to leverage our time, energy, and resources for what's in the best interest of the people and the context we find ourselves in. This definition cuts across industry, gender, age, education, and economic or social standing. Great leaders understand their responsibility to help others rise to new heights, which always benefits every endeavor. I challenge every leader I work with to remember—the higher we go in our roles and responsibilities, the more it becomes about empowering others and less about what we can achieve ourselves.

THE HERO'S JOURNEY

Years ago, I stumbled across the work of Joseph Campbell in *The Hero with A Thousand Faces* (1949). In this narratology, Campbell coins the phrase, *Hero's Journey*, to describe a wide-ranging category of stories. According to Campbell, a character enters a heroic journey to achieve something new. This character faces various conflicts, is helped by a guide, and triumphs over adversity to accomplish the mission. That mission could be to rescue the princess, destroy the Death Star, cast the ring into the fires of Mordor, win a championship as an underdog, and on and on.

Every great story in all of history follows this framework. Why? Because it is deeply imprinted in every person to move beyond our status quo and become someone better, to do something greater. Whether it's learning to play the piano, studying to become a doctor, releasing a new album, or writing a book, every new endeavor calls us into our own Hero's Journey. Great leaders understand their privilege and responsibility to serve others' Hero's Journeys.

This journey promises to challenge us to become someone different. Our identity, character, and competencies are shaped through the furnace of conflict and growth. Children seem to be on a treadmill of the Hero's Journey. They discover new things on a moment-by-moment basis, acquiring new skills, learning valuable lessons, and developing physically, mentally, and emotionally.

But something happens as we grow older. Failure becomes associated with fear, guilt, and shame, and we lose that childlike innocence and the permission to grow. Adults are supposed to have the answers and know what they're doing. Right? Little by little, we learn to project a facade of who we want others to think we are. In our longing for acceptance, we shy away from anything that could cause rejection. We overly embellish our credentials, present only flattering information about ourselves, and cautiously engage life to avoid any appearance of ignorance. Simply put, we stop taking the Hero's Journey.

Our identity, character, and competencies are shaped through *the furnace of conflict and growth.*

Picture a child learning to walk. Can you imagine what would happen every time she fell if the parent scolded the child and told her to get it right? What if every stumble solicited reactions of disapproval and rejection from the parent? We'd still be crawling our way through life! And yet, that's how so many of us feel. We have met with so many disapproving responses to our failed attempts to grow that we've become gun-shy. Most of the leaders I work with desperately want to grow but have not found a safe space to make the journey.

My own story would be radically different if there weren't mentors and coaches in my life. They gave me permission to dream bigger and to fail forward. My mentors were developmentally-minded leaders who understood that my greatest achievements would only come on the other side of stumbling and fumbling my way into a greater version of myself.

PUTTING IT ALL TOGETHER

Let me take us back to the story when a board member wanted me fired. This time I'll add more detail to demonstrate *how* and *why* EQ is so important as we seek to lead ourselves and others. At that time, I was four years into leading a thirty-eight-year-old organization through what most would call a radical rejuvenation. My arrival was met with general excitement at the prospect of how I would help this organization reach a changing world and younger generations with our services. If you've ever tried leading a group of people through any kind of change, you know what happens next. For many, the excitement of a better future quickly turned to fear, frustration and at times, full-blown rebellion as the cost of change became increasingly evident.

One of those unhappy souls was the long-standing board member I mentioned in Chapter 14. Twelve months into the transition, as things heated up for this gentleman, a showdown was inevitable. One night, he entered a board meeting with the request to share a list of concerns regarding my leadership, followed by a vote for my dismissal. I was shocked when the rest of the group agreed to let him hijack our agenda. I could not even begin to predict where this was going and how it would turn out. He spoke for over an hour, standing before the group and taping a series of papers to the wall. The board member presented a detailed account outlining his case for why I was unfit to lead this organization.

To say I wanted to jump out of my chair, cry out in my defense, and blast him in return is an understatement. I was definitely triggered! He was attacking my character, my morality, and even how I dressed! Who did this guy think he was? I could feel my temperature rise with every accusation. Quick glances from the other board members showed they were likely wondering when I would pop. I wondered the same. How much longer could I take this?

He finished, sat down, and calmly asked the board to consider my dismissal. They, in turn, looked at me and asked if I had anything to say in response. Oh, I had a lot to say! How would I respond? Should I defend myself, my reputation, my position? I clearly saw the obstacles, but where was the opportunity? I knew how I responded would either prove I was fit for this assignment or further confirm the case against me. This was yet another opportunity to practice Self-Leadership so I could be free to engage well in a highly pressurized situation.

I sat for a moment, hands deliberately folded together on the table, until all I could hear was my own breathing. Breathe in. Breathe out. Slowly. Intentionally. Again. Breathe in. Breathe out. Slowly. I took this moment to slow down, gather my thoughts, and do my best to remain composed. I wanted to be proactive and lead well in this situation, but I knew I had to lead myself first. I reminded myself that any attempt to self-protect would be seen as reactive and an expression of insecurity. I reminded myself that I had nothing to fear but missing an opportunity to learn. What if what he said was accurate? What if I'm not fit to lead this organization? It didn't matter because I was committed to being a learning leader. I believed in myself and would rather take the opportunity to discover my inadequacies than pretend I had it all figured out.

I took a deep breath and said, "I have nothing to defend. You all have seen me lead in many different situations over these past months and I'm happy to hear whether or not you share his concerns and believe they are grounds for dismissal."

Thankfully, this cantankerous individual did not find any sympathizers in the room that evening. Although other board members did share some of his concerns, they suggested he had overstepped. His personal issues with me should be re-solved privately rather than aired out as a legal hearing before the group. Multiple board members would later share with me that my humility, composure, and learning posture that evening confirmed their choice for me to lead the organization. They praised how I embodied the very leadership values we aspired to in the organization. I was far from being perfect, but they recognized my development and increased EQ. My own leadership gravitas prevailed amidst a challenge that would have turned me upside-down before.

Leading others is not about avoiding triggers, but about developing the skills of self-control so those triggers do not hijack us easily. We cannot circumvent the pinball machine of life. But we can maintain control over how we respond to the inevitable pressures that come with increasing leadership responsibility. The more we increase our leadership gravitas, the more our influence will grow.

BECOME THE GUIDE

The journey of emotional intelligence invites us to engage our own Hero's Journey so we can help others on theirs. Campbell identified brilliantly that the Hero's Journey doesn't end when we've triumphed over adversity and crossed the finish line. The Hero's Journey culminates in our willingness to *become* the guide, to leverage what we've learned to empower others on their own journey. This book is not just about your journey, but the journey I hope you will guide others on as they seek to increase their own leadership gravitas. The more you traverse the Pathway of Personal Responsibility, the more capable and confident you'll be to do the same for others. This is why we say over and over again, *You can only give to others what you have first cultivated within yourself.*

This book is intended to create space for you to fail forward and become a better version of yourself for everyone's sake. Now that you have learned the twelve core skills for practicing emotional intelligence for any and every situation you encounter, triggers, hijackings, and pinballing will no longer have the final say over your life and leadership. You now know the Pathway of Personal Responsibility, and you can choose this path whenever you want. The power is in your hands!

• EQ CHECK-IN •

1. In what ways do you see your leadership development benefitting the people you work with and the people you live with?

2. On a scale of 1-10, how confident are you to provide the necessary guidance for others on their Hero's Journey? What are you going to do about it?

3. If you were to describe your own Hero's Journey, what would it look like?

4. When you get to the end of your life, what do you hope people will say about your leadership influence in their lives?

KEY POINTS TO REMEMBER

- The higher you go in your roles and responsibilities, the more it becomes about empowering others and less about what you can achieve in and of yourself.

- Whether you are learning to play the piano, type with your fingers on the home keys, build a successful business, rise to greater roles within an organization, become a lawyer or a doctor, release a new album, write a book or a screenplay, or raise healthy kids, every new skill or endeavor calls you into your own Hero's Journey.

- Your Hero's Journey culminates in your willingness to become the guide, to leverage what you've learned in order to empower others on their own journey.

AFTERWORD:
PRACTICE MAKES BETTER

———

Throughout this book, I have offered reflective questions and short exercises to help you process the information at a personal level. These are the same ones we use week in and week out in our coaching cohorts with leaders from around the world. We've all heard it said that practice makes perfect. I prefer to say *practice makes better*. Our journey toward practicing EQ never ends. We won't arrive at perfection in this lifetime.

You have now added the EQ Matrix as a powerful tool to your arsenal. As with any tool, practice makes better. Utilize this tool as a picture or vision of your ideal leadership and assess where you are winning or struggling. Over time, this tool will become a new lens that will impact how you see everyone and every situation around you. Keep practicing the Pathway of Personal Responsibility, and you will find your leadership gravitas increasing. You will become more secure in who you are and what you are fighting for. You will become more collaborative and find greater success in partnering with others, even when they are difficult!

No matter how old you are or what you've lost on account of an EQ deficiency, it's never too late to learn these skills and become proficient in them. I have trained well-seasoned leaders who carry major organizations on their shoulders and emerging leaders looking for practical handles to begin their journey. In every case, they all agree it's worth it!

With that said, here are a few guidelines to practice going forward:

WORK ON YOURSELF FIRST

I hope by now I have drilled into your mindset that we can only give others what we first cultivate within ourselves. Too many leaders rush headlong into their responsibilities with little attention to their own development. We cannot afford to overlook the incredible importance of becoming the kind of leader others want to follow. By increasing your leadership gravitas, you will become more and more a leader worth following. Others will gravitate toward you because they're looking for a guide for their own Hero's Journey.

Give yourself permission to grow. Take regular time daily, weekly, and seasonally to reflect on your own leadership through this lens. Don't be afraid of failures. Instead, turn them on their head by choosing to learn from them. Failure will become your friend, and you will soon see that your failures have as much to teach you as your successes.

INVITE OTHERS INTO THE CONVERSATION

I strongly urge you to find some trusted partners to invite into this conversation. We need help processing what we're learning. Their thoughts, reflections, and questions will stimulate your own thinking and learning. Invite them to test the veracity of what you've learned in this book. Don't just take my word for it! Let others push and pull on these ideas and explore together whether the EQ Matrix truly paints a picture of better leadership.

I do not pretend this is a definitive work on the subject of emotional intelligence. Many books have come before this one, and many will come after. There are volumes written on each of the twelve core skills. Compare what you learn elsewhere and allow the EQ Matrix to become a tool upon which you can hang all of your learning and make sense of your experience. This tool is broad enough in scope to make room for the genius of what others have learned, while it offers us a pathway to practice the best of what we're learning in everyday life.

FIND A GROW BUDDY

Personal growth happens best with a partnership. Human beings are communal creatures. We're wired to learn with others. Find a Grow Buddy! Someone willing to create a safe place where you can be vulnerable to process the good, bad, and ugly of your leadership. You will want to find a guide who will take a vested interest in your personal transformation. This person could be a mentor, a trusted boss, a friend, a significant other.

They need to be more interested in your journey of exploration than giving you answers and solutions to the tensions that arise along the way.

Today I have many Grow Buddies. To name a few - my wife, my business partner, and my older brother all partner me in wonderful and diverse ways. With my Grow Buddies, I continue my own journey of becoming a more emotionally intelligent leader.

Months ago, I realized I was struggling more than usual to engage my own personal development. Even with these powerful tools I found it increasingly difficult to spend time intentionally practicing Self-Awareness. Because I am adamantly committed to practicing what I preach, I found a counselor who could help me dig deeper than I might with other Grow Buddies. At times we reach a point where getting unstuck from past issues can be very helpful to move forward.

GET A COACH

Finding a good leadership coach will go a long way toward helping you practice and develop your leadership gravitas and emotional intelligence. Nowadays, there are as many different types of coaches as there are needs and desires in the world. I remind my clients regularly that if the top athletes in the world seek the best coaches, then you're in good company! A good coach will help you identify your growth goals. Coaches provide high support and challenge to help you stay the course and cross the finish line into a more empowered lifestyle.

I spent years learning a variety of coaching methodologies, all of which have their place. I've worked with hundreds of organizations and thousands of leaders and have trained countless other coaches. Some of these leaders even became full-time professional coaches, while others remained within their organizations and coached from the inside. In all of this, I have learned the innumerable benefits of good coaching skills. It cannot be underestimated for those who want to take their leadership to greater heights.

A growing number of institutions offer various coaching credentials for those in search of training or a stamp of approval. Some are fantastic. Others leave much to be desired. The professional coaching industry is one of the fastest-growing of any professional industry. In many ways is still the Wild, Wild West. I don't say this lightly. What really matters is the proof in the pudding. We must find coaches with a proven track record who can provide robust testimonies of how their coaching not only led to transformation but did not leave the client codependent on the coach.

For this reason, I have made my focus training *coaching leaders.* Leaders become the best coaches of themselves and others. Good coaching doesn't just solve a problem, but it equips the client with the tools and confidence to solve their own problems.

Along with my team of well-trained coaches, we are very clear that we're not the right fit for everyone. I do believe we're the best at what we do, but I have integrity. We often counsel leaders and organizations to pursue other avenues if we are not 100% confident that the benefits from our coaching will far outweigh the time, energy, and money they will invest.

If you're not sure where to start, contact us at **www. mpwrcoaching.com** so we can help you process the best way forward for yourself, your team or organization.

THERAPY

Given what I just said, it's important to be clear. This book is not a substitute for professional counseling or therapeutic help. In your journey on the Pathway of Personal Responsibility, you will likely meet with past experiences that have deeply shaped the way you see yourself, others, and the default behaviors that keep getting you in trouble. Take a page from my notebook and if you find yourself stuck and unable to make progress with the help of a Grow Buddy, find a good counselor or therapist.

I have witnessed countless leaders over the years get incredible breakthroughs across many areas of their lives. I've seen people set free from addictions, repair broken marriages, reconcile lost relationships, rediscover their passions, and achieve what they once thought impossible. Having worked with and partnered with many mental health professionals, I have heard them regularly attest to the power of the principles and practices revealed in the EQ Matrix. But they all agree, this tool is not a substitute for professional psychiatric help.

Remember, you can only lead others to the degree that you can lead yourself. I hope to increase my leadership gravitas until the day I die, and I hope you'll join me in that endeavor.

WANT MORE?

Go to our website for additional online content at **Leadershipgravitas.com**

Made in the USA
Las Vegas, NV
07 October 2021

31898905R00125